The Way of Dialogue

The Way of Dialogue

$1 + 1 = 3$

Ronald Gordon

RESOURCE *Publications* · Eugene, Oregon

THE WAY OF DIALOGUE
1 + 1 = 3

Resource Publications
An Imprint of Wipf and Stock Publishers
199 W. 8th Ave., Suite 3
Eugene, OR 97401

www.wipfandstock.com

PAPERBACK ISBN: 978-1-5326-8510-1
HARDCOVER ISBN: 978-1-5326-8511-8
EBOOK ISBN: 978-1-5326-8512-5

Manufactured in the U.S.A.   02/07/20

"Communication liquefies all things to let new solidities emerge."

Dr. Karl Jaspers
Philosopher of Dialogue

Contents

Introduction: Heads Up! | ix

1   What is Dialogue? | 1
2   Dialogue and *I-Thou* Relating | 9
3   Our Dialogue Model: *WEG-VIBES* | 17
4   Core Communication Practices: *W-E-G* | 25
5   The Practice of Warmth | 29
6   The Practice of Empathy | 36
7   The Practice of Genuineness | 42
8   The Practice of Vulnerability | 48
9   The Practice of Imagination and Improvisation | 55
10 The Practice of Being Now and Here | 65
11 The Practice of Equality of Participation | 73
12 The Practice of Suspending | 81
13 Behind the Curtain: Dialogue Principles | 90
14 A Call to Wonder: Star-Bursting | 98
15 Check-Ins, Go-Arounds, and Quotations | 103
16 "Talk About," Sentence-Completions, and Haiku | 110
17 Mental Warm-Ups | 118
18 Returning to Awareness of Process | 123

Dialogue Observation Guide | 129
Acknowledgments | 132
Bibliography | 135
About the Author | 141

Introduction: Heads Up!

FOR DECADES I'VE BEEN a professor of communication on the Hilo campus of the University of Hawai'i teaching our department's seminar in human dialogue (as well as classes in interpersonal communication and senior-level courses in listening, leadership, and communication and love). I will now teach you what I teach my students about dialogue, because especially in today's world of divisiveness and incivility, we all need to know more about the way of dialogue.

It's important to have a guiding model when pursuing the way of dialogue, and in these pages you'll receive grounding in our **WEG-VIBES** dialogue model. This user-friendly model summarizes what gets us to dialogue. About 40 percent of this dialogue model emerges from the *person-centered* approach (PCA) made famous by Dr. Carl Rogers,[1] and the remainder derives from dialogue theory and research.[2] In the next few readings we'll talk more about what a *person-centered* approach to dialogue means.

Also woven throughout these pages is encouragement to practice breath awareness. The ancient practice of breath awareness has been in existence for literally thousands of years in cultures around our world. For the past three decades, mindfulness of breathing has also received major scientific study here in the West. Breath awareness has stood both the test of time and the tests of science. Proven to be a tremendous tool for self-soothing and self-regulation, it can also can handily assist us in effectively activating each of our **WEG-VIBES** dialogue practices that you'll learn about.

I will focus on breath awareness in this *Introduction* because it's such an integral strand in this book, and runs throughout. I want to give you advance notice that these pages are designed to not just speak to your brain alone, but to speak to your breathing body as well. You're being invited to

1. Rogers and Russell, *Quiet Revolutionary.*
2. Anderson et al., *Reach of Dialogue.*

become an embodied learner in the art of dialogue. The more you learn to use your breathing as a mindfulness tool that can help you skillfully finesse your way through sometimes challenging human conversations, the better off everyone will be.

Yes, our breathing process is vital for keeping us alive, but we can also learn to turn our breathing process (which we engage in about 20,000 times a day) into one of our closest friends and strongest allies in this world. This will serve us well on the frontlines of our daily communication efforts with other people.

For about four decades I've lived far out in the Pacific Ocean on the multicultural Big Island of Hawai'i, almost halfway to Asia. As a result across the years I've become steeped in ancient East Asian wisdom, and often call upon it in my teaching. For example, in *The Secret of the Golden Flower* it is said, "Worldly people lose the roots, and cling to the tree-tops."[3]

Breath awareness in this book is our way of getting down from the tree-tops and back to being deeply rooted. Practicing breath awareness can enable us to sink our attention down beneath our head and anchor ourselves more mindfully in our body's actual center, down in our abdominal region, in order to become more grounded, stabilized, and balanced.

Our awareness of our deep bodily breathing can drop us beneath our chattering left brain hemisphere and into our wiser lower torso "center-mind." At times turning to our logical brain isn't enough, or takes too long, and we need to more quickly call upon other of our organism's capacities. This is where our practice of breath awareness comes in, a stabilizing tool that we can easily learn to use and that's constantly available to us.

Following our breathing for less than a handful of breaths can help us begin to decrease our blood pressure and rate of respiration, lower our production of stress hormones, minimize our attachment to disruptive emotions, and reduce our rate of impulsive behavioral reactivity. Breath awareness also serves as a form of mental training, strengthening our capacity for consciously directing our attention to wherever we choose for it to go.[4] In short, our physical and mental health, and our self-awareness and self-management, are all up-leveled through our mindful breath awareness,[5] as well as our ability to more skillfully implement each of the foundational **WEG-VIBES** dialogue practices.

3. Wilhelm and Jung, *Golden Flower*, 69.

4. Goleman and Davidson, *Altered Traits*, Ch. 5.

5. Brown et al., *Handbook of Mindfulness*.

If practicing breath awareness will be new to you, welcome aboard. My students consistently give vivid before-and-after testimonials in my classes as to what a striking difference the practice of breath awareness makes in their communication, and in their daily lives. For more than twenty years I've heard these firsthand personal reports, and the existing scientific literature echoes such reports with experimental validity and reliability.

And if you're already doing a breath awareness practice, excellent, with the approach here you'll deepen your practice, and start to smoothly blend it into your excursions into *person-centered* dialogue.

Eckhart Tolle was once asked which specific courses he would recommend at an upcoming personal development symposium, and he replied, "Be aware of your breathing as often as you are able, whenever you remember. Do that for one year, and it will be more powerfully transformative than attending all these courses. And it's free."[6]

There's by now ample scientific research to warrant such a recommendation. And here's the good news: ***I've used a special device in this book*** to enable you to conveniently become aware of, enjoy, and constructively use your breathing process as a tool to help you activate the core practices of the art of dialogue.

Here's the heads-up:

Every time from here on out in these pages whenever you see the phrase Slow Down, Stand Back, See More, and Step Forth Wisely (and its variations), feel your body slowly and deeply breathing in, and out, for four complete breath cycles, while inwardly repeating this key power-phrase to yourself.

This power-phrase is meant to be a print signal to you, a cue, an invitation to right at that moment close your eyes, and to actually feel (and not just think about) your breath coming into your nostrils, deep down into your torso, and out your mouth, as you silently utter our key phrase.

Ideally, take one breath in and out on "Slow Down," another breath in and out on "Stand Back," another in and out on "See More," and a fourth complete breath cycle on "Step Forth Wisely." But especially when this is new to you, if you don't quite synchronize breath and words in this way, it's okay. The main thing is to bodily *feel* four deep breaths, in and out, as you silently repeat our key phrase. It's *feeling* your body *breathing* that matters most.

How can experiencing breath awareness ever be of use to us during dialogue? Here's but one example: whenever we want to minimize having an overly defensive and nasty verbal *reaction* to what someone else has said

6. Tolle, *A New Earth*, 244.

or done and instead glide into a more skillful *response*, we would do well to slide our awareness down into *feeling our breathing body* in that instant, and at the same time silently repeat our short verbal formula within ourselves: *Slow Down, Stand Back, See More, Step Forth Wisely.*

This can slow the tempo of events, and provide precisely the buffer we need for incoming brain signals to advance up beyond our brain's limbic system and reach our prefrontal cortex, where our rationality resides. This breath awareness and power-phrase can often provide us with just enough of a pause to make wiser choices in that all-important space between "stimulus" and "response," which is where our human freedom is born.

The first three micro-stages, *Slow Down, Stand Back, See More*, are to provide pause, perspective, and vision. The fourth stage, *Step Forth Wisely*, is to prime the stage of skillful response, whether such a response entails listening patiently and fully, or choosing our words carefully and side-stepping conflict, or otherwise artfully responding. We eventually learn to synchronize our mental utterance of our key phrase with our breathing, *feeling one in-breath and one out-breath during each of the four phrase-stages.*

We can call our key power-phrase a verbal reminder, a useful formula, an affirmation, or a mantra. What we call this verbal tool doesn't matter as much as actually using it, combined with four deep breaths, to facilitate sliding into our each of our **WEG-VIBES** dialogue practices with enhanced ease.

Too often in conversation we let stiff and rigid states of mind-and-body dictate our reactions. In these pages we're going to practice internally re-setting ourselves, coming back to our roots, using breath awareness combined with our key power-phrase as our secret leveraging device (and by "secret" I mean that no one else needs to know we're using it, unless we want them to).

So I invite you to jumpstart your practice of breath awareness by becoming aware of your breathing and *feeling* it each time you see our empowering phrase printed on the page. How about doing this again now, even if you've already done it above? Read our four-part phrase as you let your body slowly inhale and exhale four times, and *feel* your body breathing all along the way: *Slow Down, Stand Back, See More, Step Forth Wisely.* Go ahead, I'll wait.

Good for you.

Feeling at least slightly better than 20 or so seconds ago?

Chances are your answer is "Yes."

And if it's not, as we continue on, it soon will be.

In every reading in these pages I've included this power-phrase (or a close variation) once or more: *Slow Down, Stand Back, See More, Step Forth Wisely.* These wise words are meant to serve as a print-cue to you, a reminder you're being invited, at that instant, to take a 20 to 30 second pause (no big deal) and close your eyes, silently repeat our special phrase, while feeling your body breathing. Then open your eyes, and continue on with your reading.

Neuroimaging brain research shows that it's not *mentally* remembering you're breathing that's the important element here, it's actually *feeling* the sensations of your living body as it's breathing.[7] Out of the mind, into the body; below the head and brain and neck and into the torso, down closer to our bodily center, our abdominal region, and what's been called "center-mind."

Out of the tree tops, back to our roots.

Ultimately up to you, but if you do choose to accept this breath awareness invitation repeatedly as you read this book, I guarantee rewards will come. I've used a similar *print-based breathing practice cue* in my book *On Becoming an Attuned Communicator* for a decade,[8] and over 80 percent of my students say they regularly accept the breath awareness invitation as they read that book, and that doing so positively impacts their life and communication. They frequently find it more powerful than any other single tool or concept to which they're introduced.

Thich Nhat Hanh colorfully expresses the intimate relationship between breathing, body, and mind as follows: "When you breathe in, the air enters your body and calms all the cells of your body. At the same time, each 'cell' of your breathing becomes more peaceful, and each 'cell' of your mind becomes more peaceful. Body, breathing, and mind are one, and each one is all three."[9]

During a dialogue, we can move into each of our eight **WEG-VIBES** dialogue practices more effortlessly with the subtle assistance of our mindful breath awareness. The faster we drive in a vehicle the more our field of vision narrows; and, conversely, our field of vision expands as we slow down. We're decelerating and feeling our breathing so that we can enlarge our field of vision and our options for positive communication action.

7. Smalley and Winston, *Fully Present*, Ch. 3.

8. Gordon, revised 2018 edition titled *Tuning-In: The Art of Mindful Communicating.*

9. Nhat Hanh, *Breathe, You Are Alive*, 55.

We're learning to experience our breathing and calm ourselves down as an ongoing integral component of our dialogue practice.

Please consider yourself heartily encouraged to discover more of the way of dialogue in these pages, and invited to catch the dialogical spirit. Your steps toward building havens of true dialogue will be appreciated by those around you, both in your personal and professional lives. Time to make the world, or even a small piece of it, a better place, starting from where we are.

Let's first ask: what is dialogue?

1

What is Dialogue?

WHEN WE LOOK AT common everyday usages of the word "dialogue" we find that the word usually means something different from what it means in this book.

For example, "Dialogue refers to lines spoken by characters in a work of fiction." True enough, but that's not the kind of dialogue we're talking about here.

Or, "Dialogue is a conversation between two persons or more." Nope, not all everyday conversations are dialogues, not the way most dialogue scholars use this term, and not as we'll use it either. Here dialogue is viewed as a form of conversational curiosity guided by certain core practices, but when these core practices and a sincere questing curiosity are lacking, then we don't label that conversation as being of "dialogical" quality just because two or more people were talking. That's insufficient to warrant this special qualitative term.

Or, "Dialogue is a reasoned debate between two or more parties to a conflict." The mass media regularly portray dialogue as having a debate-like format, but that's not how we're employing our key term in these pages. Debate is basically a controlled verbal contest between two opposing sides, both behaving as if they're "right" while the other side is "wrong." Strategic manipulation, deception, combative semantic-slanting and name-calling, all this and more is often part of the debate game. But debate and dialogue are not equivalent. Dialoguing is *not* about advocating and persuading, defending and attacking, decimating and destroying, winning and losing.

Or, "Dialogue is a discussion intended to produce a negotiated agreement." While often depicted this way on the world stage of diplomacy, it's not our meaning here. Dialoguing, as we conceive of it, is *not* about narrowing down a set of ideas or proposals and eliminating options as problem-solving discussion would have us do. And dialoguing is *not* about negatively depicting other positions and persons along the way in an effort to make sure that our position prevails.

So what *is* dialogue?

Shared inquiry is at the very heart of dialoguing; it's what dialogue is about, at least in our usage of our key term. We have a conversation in which we experience what it means to be truly *inquiring together* into a topic area: wondering about it out loud together, teasing it out, shedding new light on it, raising questions about it, reflecting upon it together. Our dialogical conversation essentially proceeds in the mode of the question mark, rather than in the mood of the strong period, the exclamation point, and the pointed finger.

As well, in dialogical conversation our tone of voice and facial expressions can be supportive of our dialogue partners; we don't win any points for being sarcastic, rejecting, harsh, and shaming, nor would we want to be. In authentic dialogue our goodwill toward others is apparent, and we work to steer clear of succumbing to mean-spiritedness. This is not a competitive sport we're playing: we're not looking to demolish an opponent, and what we believe they stand for. There are no opponents in this conversation.

We're dialogue partners and we're on the same side, together looking outward. Dialogue is on our horizon. We use our conversational energies to work together to pursue the way of dialoguing. I will use the word "together" repeatedly in these pages, because being together in joint inquiry is at the nucleus of the *person-centered* dialogue process: we connect inter-*personally* as we feel, think, and create, all in a spirit of collaborative and trans-active inquiry.

In *person-centered* dialoguing we stand shoulder-to-shoulder united in inquiry, not shouting and staring each other down with ill-temper. *Person-centered* dialogue is not *position-centered* debate or discussion where our allegiance is to a fixed argumentative stance and where we vigorously *defend* our position against onslaught as we *attack* the opposition. That kind of *position-centered* debate or discussion format can go from impersonal to downright de-humanizing. As one observer put it, "I'm amazed by the ease with which people belittle one another these days, as if it were a reasonable thing to do." We've maybe been there ourselves; now we're moving on.

Person-centered dialoguing asks us to continually return to an embodied awareness of the *humanity* of our dialogue partners. As we seek to engage in shared inquiry we treat our dialogue partners as eminently worthy of our respect and understanding. We're also aware of the distinct entity that is our actual *relationship* with our dialogue partners, and we recognize, dignify, and honor our unique inter*personal relationship*.

As we uncover what it means to be literally *thinking together* we at the same time set out to treat the other persons, ourselves, and our relationship with *Unconditional Positive Regard, Empathy,* and *Genuineness.* These are the three core practices within the *person-centered* approach to dialogue. The *person-centered* approach to human relationships in general was developed by the eminent psychologist Dr. Carl Rogers, whose thinking we'll soon get to in greater detail.[1]

Most of what goes under name "dialogue" in our popular culture is *not* characterized by *Unconditional Positive Regard, Empathy,* and *Genuineness,* but *person-centered* dialoguing does strive to put these three major elements into practice. The personhood of the other persons and ourselves is held high as we explore topics and questions before us in a mood of honest curiosity. This book's vision and practice of dialoguing emanates, then, from the *person-centered* school of thought, and you will begin to soak up this vision from the words on these pages.

In *person-centered* dialoguing we seek to open-up rather than close-down ourselves and others both as communicators and persons, while we actively explore our thinking and feeling around meaningful topics. Right about now maybe an embodied visual image will help to convey the primary difference between discussion/debate, and dialogue. It's worthwhile when we take certain concepts not only into the left hemisphere of our brain but into more of the rest of our body and mind as well.

So place your hands in front of you, palms together, fingertips pointing forward, away from you. Now keep your fingertips touching as you move the heels of your palms three or four inches apart. You are basically making an arrow, pointing outward from your body, about like this: >.

This arrow represents the trajectory of standard *position-centered* discussion and debate, everything getting reduced down to a small point at the far end. The aim is to dismiss alternatives and finally arrive at a single surviving position, a decision, the best answer, "the winner." Folks start out with lots of stuff being said, slugging it out with their alleged facts, theories, stories, statistics, examples, images, slanted semantics, and see what proposed solution or answer is finally left standing by the end: >.

The field gets winnowed until eventually "done deal," something and someone survives the ordeal and is declared the victor. Options are

1. Rogers, *A Way of Being.*

3

reduced, and not uncommonly so are persons. Incivility tends to occur, often nasty verbal swipes and stabs. At times it can become downright brutal, ugly, injurious, and ethically unfit as vigorous attempts are made to destroy the opposition's positions, and even the opposition. Toxicity often fouls the ethical climate.

Now put your palms together once again. This time instead of separating from the thumb pad end of your palms, separate your two hands at the fingertip end (the opposite end from before), letting your extended fingers of the left and right hands be six or seven or eight inches apart. There's a wide opening at the outer end this time, the fingertip end rather the palm end. It's again a "V" of sorts, but now with the openness facing outward. This flying "V" represents what it means to be dialoguing: <.

Position-centered debate and discussion, as traditionally practiced, often hammer-down positions and persons, while our approach to dialoguing is about the stretching and broadening of persons and possibilities. With *person-centered* dialoguing we're roaming terrain together, wondering, telling our stories, disclosing, laughing, thinking tentatively with one another, imagining, reaching, risking, reflecting, creating, learning. Our flying "V" forges forward and upward, our motion more like this: <.

Dialogue, as this term is used here, doesn't set out to shut down, put down, and close-off possibilities and persons like *position-centered* discussion or debate so frequently tend to do. In *person-centered* dialoguing we're not dismissing choices and dissing human beings, we're sincerely pursuing genuine open-ended inquiry together. Dialoguing enlarges and cultivates persons and topics, it's about widening and fanning-out. We often end-up with more questions than we had at the beginning, and no final answers, yet we feel uplifted because of our shared consciousness-expanding exploration.

As a result of our dialoguing we feel enriched, we feel good about each other, and we look forward to more of this type of conversation in the future. We've been mentally and emotionally stirred and enriched by our cooperative and sincere search within our chosen topic areas, and we're all the better for having had our dialogical conversation. We've been discovering the art of *thinking together*, not only independently, and this makes its impact upon us.

Person-centered dialoguing, then, involves open-ended respectful conversation conducted in a legitimate spirit of inquiry. This form of dialoguing entails exploratory wonderment in a non-combative and humane inter*personal* atmosphere. Open-ended dialoguing can involve two people or two dozen people. Again, it's not the quantity of participants that defines dialogue: *it's the quality of shared interpersonal inquiry that makes a given conversation more, or less, dialogical.*

Humans are ultra-cooperative as a species, and highly collaborative at the group level. We know how to subordinate "me" to "we" and function together interdependently and harmoniously: ancestrally been there, done that. The way of collaborative dialoguing of the sort we're talking about in these pages calls upon us to awaken and employ this innate capacity for "we" in our communication with others. We wonder and wander together, side-by-side, exploring the content before us, and that emerges from within us, and between us.

Person-centered dialoguing is about fusion energy, *you* and *me* fusing as *we*, and working with one another to inquire into the nature and layers and facets of something. But we're not just working, we're often playing too, we're tossing around a beach ball, or a few beach balls, in the waves. We're throwing, reaching, diving, leaping, catching, and gaining insights together. Instead of functioning as individual particles, together we become more wave-like.

Collaborative *person-centered* dialoguing is 1 + 1 = 3, with the whole becoming greater than the sum of its parts. Dialogue takes two or five or ten or twenty brains and gets them talking and feeling and *thinking together* about some topics, piggybacking and bouncing off one another's contributions, building community, exponentially multiplying human brainpower, synergistically raising our collective IQ and EQ (our mental and emotional intelligences). We fan-out our minds, we open our awareness and our hearts in togetherness, and surprise ourselves.

In 1 + 1 = 3 we yield to hunches, flashes, mini-stories, disclosures, conjectures, humor, and we're frequently off-the-cuff, out-of-the-box, and off-the-wall. We are getting the feel of truly *thinking together*. We interdependently ferret out discoveries, coming up with more than any of us would have alone; this is to be dialoguing.

Such dialoguing is about moments of "authentic meeting" among persons, an acute flow-through of life energies as we together search the surfaces, depths, and heights of a topic. Our conversations at such moments of authentic meeting and minding can take on a life of their own, and nurture us at levels of mind, body, heart, spirit, and relationship.

There is no single bottom-line; our dialoguing has positive effects simultaneously on multiple levels.

The expression "a dialogue" used as a noun can sound excessively static, like dialogue is "a thing" (an object) with a beginning, middle, and end, like "a speech" or "an essay." The verb forms "to dialogue" or "to be dialoguing" capture more of the momentariness of what it means to dialogue, more of its status as "a happening" rather than a long-lasting and rigidly demarcated entity. Our dialoguing is happening when our popcorn is popping, and fills and fulfills us.

Yes, there are times when we humans benefit from well-handled discussion and the fission of debate, when we need to skillfully clash positions, weigh alternative proposals, jettison weak ones, and select a single best course of belief and action. There are times for artful advocacy, cleanly and soundly executed. There's no question about the importance of, and need for, articulate and ethical advocacy and persuasion in our society and world.

But we often rush to judgment prematurely. We push one another too quickly to narrow-down, and we get defensive and tacky and petty before we've sufficiently widened our thinking and entertained an expanding array of seed images, insights, and speculative scenarios. There are times when wisdom would have us postpone reductive discussion or hard-edged heated debate and instead proceed for a while in a mood of innocent curiosity. We may need to get to more fully know ourselves and one another first, and build bridges upon which we can stand together and look around.

In this endeavor it can help if we start to become aware of our breathing, and smoothly begin to *Slow Down* a little, as we finally take a moment to catch our breath; and *Stand Back* inside ourselves, and take pleasure in this breathing we now reclaim; and maybe we can begin to *See More* as we slowly breathe and let go a little, relaxing our structure ever so slightly; and then, we can perhaps breathe a sigh of relief and restoration, and gradually start to *Step Forth Wisely.*

Dr. David Bohm, one of the founding deans of modern dialogue, said that as we dialogue we need no agenda, no hierarchy, no definitive purpose aside from the *spirit of inquiry* and the creation of an *open free space* where we can let anything be explored *without negative judgment.* He depicted dialoguing as "a free-flowing" of ideas and meanings, without fears of disapproval and rejection.[2]

2. Bohm, *On Dialogue*, Ch. 2.

There are times to avoid shrinking and shriveling to this > and instead be reaching for this <. The world can benefit from less polarizing and de-personalizing *position-centered* debate and discussion, and from an ascendance of exploratory *person-centered* dialogue as we advance yet further into the twenty-first century. Our well-being, and very survival, might depend upon the cultivation of precisely our capacity to expand persons and parameters.

For this to best happen we need to learn certain core practices and principles so that we can pursue and sustain the way of dialoguing. The mind has many "channels," and in this book we're tuning-in to the *person-centered* and *inquiry-based* dialogue channel rather than the *position-centered* and *advocacy-based* debate and discussion channel.

Our next reading will address this question: what mindset do we look out from when we want to develop conversations with others that dip more deeply into the dialogical? We'll gradually learn to move away from low-road and often depersonalizing, demeaning, and even destructive alternating monologues, and instead begin to travel together, at long last, on the way of dialoguing.

Through dialoguing we're reaching for *Encounters of the Fourth Kind*: deep and significant contact and connection with other terrestrial beings.

Taking Action

This week, listen and look all around you: in the media, in your family, at work, with friends, in public places, and notice how often people are trying to make others seem off-base, lacking in facts or good sense, or somehow just plain "wrong." Witness *advocacy* all around.

Also notice how rarely this attempted persuasion effort succeeds, how most folks resist being negated or made "wrong," and they either outwardly or inwardly try to fight back. Casually observe how conversations get road-blocked or dead-ended because of the ways people react to one another in these everyday advocacy-oriented conversations.

Look, listen, learn.

There is much lesson here, especially on what *not* to do.

And as you immerse yourself in the words in these chapters allow internal rigidities to automatically tenderize themselves, easing tightened mental and physical structures, relieving yourself of these burdens,

THE WAY OF DIALOGUE

becoming receptive to whatever it is that you need to more completely realize, taking it to heart, and then into your center of wisdom.

Reflecting

*I realize that the ways of conventional discussion and debate often lead to
problems, breakdowns, and failed potentials. If I'm open-minded to learning
about the way of dialogue what do I have to lose? What do I have to gain?
How will I know until I step forth?*

*As a starter, in my own and other peoples' interactions this week do
I witness much interrupting, dogmatizing, polarizing, controlling, attacking, defending, manipulating, along with the use of sarcasm, ridicule, and
contempt?*

*Or, am I witnessing genuine shared wondering, listening, reflecting, cre-
ating, synthesizing, and people essentially thinking together?*

*What do I see and hear all around me: position-centered grappling and
kickboxing, or person-centered shared inquiry, where people are sharing and
thinking together?*

2

Dialogue and *I-Thou* Relating

THE LATE DR. MARTIN Buber is a dialogue giant. He was a twentieth century philosophy professor at Hebrew University in Jerusalem, and to this day remains a major figure in dialogue scholarship and practice. In 1919 he wrote one of his most famous books, *I and Thou*. This small and highly valued work has been translated into dozens of languages, and continues to influence dialogue scholars and practitioners all around the world.[1]

Professor Buber's writings are not easy to read, but his intensity of pursuit is captivating. He dedicated his life to thinking about how we humans might go beyond endless *monologue* where we each merely talk *at* each another. He aspired to teach true dialogue where we have respectful personal encounters *with* one another on substantial topics of deep personal inquiry.

The approaches of Martin Buber and Carl Rogers, two leading figures in the art of *person-centered* dialogue, take us toward the heart of the psychological and emotional climate conducive to dialoguing. They help us reduce the likelihood of *Moving Against* one another in conversation, or psychologically and emotionally *Moving Away* from each other, and increase the probability that we'll *Move Toward* and *Move With* one another in constructive dialoguing.

Dr. Buber says there's one huge key choice that we each have to make repeatedly in our daily lives. To have any hopes of achieving true dialogue, we need to grasp the difference between what Buber describes as the impersonal *I-It* mode of perceiving and relating as compared against the more personal *I-Thou* way of relating with others. At any given moment we can existentially *choose* to stand in *I-It* relation to the person we're talking to, or have an *I-Thou* relation with them. [2]

1. Buber, *I and Thou*.
2. Buber, *I and Thou*, Part I.

This "two-fold" choice stands in front of us always. Everything else follows from this fundamental choice that we usually make non-consciously. As students of dialogue we become increasingly aware of which choices we are making with whom, and when. We become more attentive to what modality we're choosing in any given instance, *I-It* or *I-Thou*, and soon come to have greater influence over this customarily outside-of-awareness choice-making.

When we treat a person as an *It* we're basically treating them as an object, as a "thing." We label them as belonging to this or that gender category, this or that race, culture, political party, age group, religion, personality type, ethnicity, occupation, fraternity, sorority, geographical location, socio-economic status, or whatever.

We then turn to the file folder in our mind into which we can file this other ("they're another one of those, that's what they are"), and deal with them expeditiously. We de-personalize the other and don't see them as an individual human being, but instead stereotype them based upon the demographic categories and groups by which they can be labeled. Then we react to them as we do to most other objects in that category.

So sometimes we treat others as *Its*. This is handy, quick, and it helps us preserve order in our minds and deal with the *Its* of this world in an efficient manner, or so we tell ourselves. This stereotyping allows us to manage an otherwise complex social reality. It works well enough for us when we're in a hurry, so we rely on it. We humans tend to be cognitive misers; we like mental shortcuts that spare us physical, mental, and emotional labor.

On the other hand, treating another person as a *Thou* and standing in *I-Thou* relation with them is quite different. We take the time to look past the person's similarities to others, past the groups into which we can pigeonhole them, past the stereotypes that could conceivably be applied, and we begin to see them as *person*. We especially begin to see them in their *uniqueness* and their *immeasurability*. These are two of the primary qualities that we can start to look for and intentionally focus upon when we want to transition from *I-It* to *I-Thou* perception.[3]

Uniqueness. When we see someone as *Thou*, we remind ourselves that they are not duplicated by any other person on this planet, there is only one of them, they are literally non-interchangeable. We know that their fingerprints, their voiceprints, their pupil patterns, their specific brain configurations, their DNA, their inner physiological and chemical landscape, their

3. Buber, *I and Thou*, Part II.

personality structure, their exact appearance, and so much more is theirs and theirs alone.

And certainly no one else in this world has gone through the totally same set of life experiences and in identical sequence as has this person in front of us. No, no one else is an exact duplicate of precisely this specific human being. Even identical twins are not equivalent (and especially when they choose not to be).

Once we reach out to catch the flavor of the non-interchangeability of a particular human being, their true *uniqueness*, they become special to us. We begin to treat them less as *It* and more as *Thou*. We start to honor them in their *uniqueness*, to celebrate them as a one-of-a-kind original, we honor their particularity. We go past merely paying lip service to them being a *unique* phenomenon in this universe, and ourselves experience this bodily and emotionally. We allow our heart to be touched by our embodied sensing of this person's factual *uniqueness*.

We also recognize and appreciate what this other person shares in common with other human beings, including their capacities to imagine, choose, communicate, create, aspire, and grow. We value the powerful combination of both their *shared humanity* and their *personal uniqueness*. Again, with this felt recognition our heart opens at least slightly more, and maybe a lot more.

Immeasurability. When we see another person as a *Thou* we also realize they're ultimately *immeasurable*. No matter how many observations and analyses we could conceivably make about the other person, we will never have said it all. We can measure them this way and that, yes, but in the final analysis this person will always exceed our ability to summarize them in language and numbers. It is not that they are *un-measurable*, but that they are ultimately *immeasurable*.

As Professor Buber suggests to us, "Nothing else is present but this one, but this one cosmically. Measure and comparison have fled. *It is up to you how much of the immeasurable becomes reality for you*" (italics added).[4] If we but have the eyes to see, the other person can even become sacred mystery. To start to sense this, we become aware of feeling our breathing in this immediate moment as we also ever so gently *Slow Down*; and then we take another breath in, and out, as we *Stand Back*; and then we breathe in and out again, as we come to *See More*; and finally we complete one more breath cycle, in and out, as we prepare ourselves to *Step Forth Wisely*.

4. Buber, *I and Thou*, 83.

When we open ourselves to the *Thou* dimensions of this other person, to sensing their *uniqueness* and *immeasurability*, then we, and they, feel our heightened quality of interpersonal perception. Martin Buber says usually we skim across the surface of people rather than really encountering them, yet the potential exists for entering into true relation with the other and receptively beholding them. It is our existential freedom to choose to go beyond thinking in terms of "thing-hood," and instead consecrate living systems through our enhanced richer vision. Dr. Buber recommends this to us, "For as soon as we touch a *Thou*, we are touched by a breath of eternal life."[5]

We often fail to do this because we think there is nothing much out there that we haven't already seen and heard before. But Buber cautions us to first look within ourselves: "Often we think there is nothing to be heard, as if we had not long ago plugged wax into our own ears."[6] Dr. Buber says that once we do begin to behold the other in their *uniqueness* and *immeasurability*, then we actualize their and our living presence: "Only as the *Thou* becomes present, does presence come into being."[7] The deeper we see and feel, the more we wake up and come to life.

There is a striking contrast between relating to another as an *It* or a *Thou*. To see them as an *It* is quick and easy, to be sure, yet dismissive of so much. It gets us sorting through people speedily so we can move right along, but much therefore goes unseen, unheard, and unknown. The price for our speed is loss of richness of vision, knowledge, and understanding.

Each time we have a conversation with someone this week we will make this *fundamental choice*, either treating this other person more as an *It*, or more as *Thou*. This choice is ours each and every encounter. We would do well to start becoming mindfully aware of the choice we are about to make, are now making, or did make:

I-It _____ *I-Thou*

Again, I remind you that the subtle practice of breath awareness can advance us on this *I-Thou* continuum. As we listen to another person speak, we can *Slow Down* as we take-in deep breath #1, and then quietly release this breath. We can *Stand Back* inside ourselves on breath #2 as we smoothly inhale and exhale. We can delicately *See More* as we feel breath #3

5. Buber, *I and Thou*, 113.
6. Buber, *I and Thou*, 182.
7. Buber, *I and Thou*, 63.

coming into, and going out of, our body. Then on breath #4 we smoothly *Step Forth Wisely* in more skillful response, however this might take shape in the present moment. We often pleasantly surprise ourselves.

Our four deep breathings along with our mental phrase *Slow Down, Stand Back, See More, Step Forth Wisely* can be an incredibly strong ally here. They can be of value in permitting us to gently transition from an *I-It* way of reductively labelling and treating the other person to a deeper *I-Thou* experiencing, coming from, as Buber puts it, our "whole being."

We receive this other person in their *Thou-ness*, and let our senses, dimensions, and open-heartedness awaken. Elevation occurs for both perceiver and perceived.

We would do well across our interactions this day and this week to ask ourselves at moments: "Where am I about to place, and then treat, this other person on the *I-It* to *I-Thou* continuum?" We slow down, and subtly breathe our way into at least slightly further movement in the *I-Thou* direction.

This is possible, and can be done.

We're all busy people, of course, and maybe don't always have the time and inclination to slow down and make the *I-Thou* choice. We're not saints, we're flawed human beings and often in a hurry and under stress.

Yet at other times the *I-Thou* choice is clearly the best course of action, and doable.

We simply start to notice with greater clarity how we're seeing and choosing at any given moment. The word "respect" comes from the Latin word *respecere*, "to look again." To move into *I-Thou* seeing we "double-take" again and again with eyes of resilience and surprise. We know there is always more to invite, find, and experience as insightful and invaluable.

We humbly listen to the highs and lows, the bends and turns of this person's life stories, the assumptive world out of which they function. We become repeatedly willing to receive again, with fresh eyes and ears, each time seeing and hearing more deeply. We come to *respect* this other person for who they are as a *unique* and ultimately *immeasurable* human being, for what they've already been through in their lifetime, and for where they might yet be headed. We behold and hallow the other; we hold them high in our head and heart.

Communication that follows from viewing the other as an *It* is usually impersonal communication, while communication that flows from an *I-Thou* relation feels more like inter*personal* communication. For open-ended dialoguing to flourish we need to grow beyond heavy reliance on *I-It* detachment and slide into *I-Thou* receptivity. The recurring question becomes, "Am I treating this person now in front of me impersonally as an *It*, or am I treating them inter*personally* as *Thou*?"

It can seem to us at first glance that some folks are just "average" people, but the fact is we've never met a statistically "average" human being in our entire life (e.g., we've never met a parent with 1.36 children and 1.78 family cars). We only see "average" because of where we're perceiving from, and Buber provides us with a leveraging device for changing our angle of perception and our mindset.

In our wiser moments when we have our wits about us we can choose to feel our breathing, and silently and inwardly utter our phrase *Slow Down, Stand Back, See More*, and *Step Forth Wisely*. With the enhanced awareness this brings we can then move out of auto-pilot mode and, all the better, into authentic inter*personal* connection.

Albert Einstein famously said "The most beautiful thing we can experience is the mysterious."[8] Our practice of mindful and subtle breath awareness can be instrumental in our refined sensing of this other human being's *uniqueness* and *immeasurability* and vibrantly participating in their mysteriousness. Everyone benefits, and so does our collaborative *person-centered* dialoguing. We get personal, and gates open wide to profound connectedness and free-flowing conversation.

One of my favorite communication scholars, the late Dr. Bud Goodall of Arizona State University, recalled his earliest encounter back in high school with what he later came to realize had been a dialogical adventure: "We got into things neither one of us had ever spoken about to anyone else, and I know for a fact that there were things we talked about that I had not even thought about before. I know my heart was pumping fast too, and by the time we came to the end of it, more an arrival than a destination, we were both exhausted but knew we had been somewhere special together. I remember the stars that night, the moon, the feel of the air, everything around us was alive and deeply meaningful. And I'll never forget, because I've spent so much of my life since then trying to get there again. Trying to find that special place where true communication happens."[9]

Dr. Goodall late in his career passionately wrote about "dialogic moments as pathways to peak experiences." I know what he was talking about.

8. Einstein, *Living Philosophies*.
9. Goodall, Jr. and Kellett, "Pathways to Peak Experiences," 160.

Dialogue is often considered a type of conversation that rises us up above the mundane and takes us into what feels like the realm of the "transcendent." This quality of conversation is beyond the norm, it exceeds the average; it's special, and makes its own lasting impact upon us.

Dialoguing, rightly practiced, has Power and Spirit. This Power can stir us to life and this dialogical Spirit can awaken us to shared human intimacy of mind and heart. In this way dialoguing can touch us profoundly and remain as part of who we become as human beings. We inter-connect with others and fulfill more of the meaningfulness of life.

This book is meant to offer a helping hand in getting us to this satisfying and healing place as we journey the way of *person-centered* dialoguing.

Taking Action

Across your days become more aware of how you're looking out at others. Are you placing them on the *I-It* side of the continuum, or on the *I-Thou* side? What *fundamental choice* are you making at any given moment?

Become receptive to the other's *uniqueness* by making it your focused intention to do so, to see yet further into this human being across from you. *Slowing Down* and *Standing Back* can definitely help us *See More*, and then ultimately we can *Step Forth Wisely*, especially as we *feel* our body breathing all along the way. We let this become second nature. We're taking mere seconds of clock time, literally, to engage in this repeated practice of breath awareness as we read, and as we dialogue. We be good to our Selves in this way, and at the same time invest in our healthy communication present and future with others.

As we sit or stand across from another person we open our warm heart and mind to more of this person's *immeasurability* with our inhalations, and we breathe in more of their totality, while knowing there's always more than we will ever have eyes to completely plumb. "As I breathe in, I breathe in more of my partner's *immeasurability*. And as I breathe out, I breathe out any limiting images and stereotypes." We can say this silently two or three times as we quietly breathe and listen to our dialogue partner.

We celebrate the ultimate sacred mystery of this specific other person. We softly reach into their being with our mind and heart. This is a mind-set and a body-set move, an internal shifting, a melting of rigid mental categories and structures, and instead softening into a respectful and life-enhancing mood and mode of *Fascination*.[10]

We choose to reach out with our imagination and intelligent intuition and allow our Self to become *Fascinated*, to take a whiff of the other's *uniqueness* and ultimate *immeasurability*.

We welcome our Self, and others, into these openings into Being together.

Reflecting

What do I become aware of as I begin noticing those times when I treat others more as an It, or, instead, as a Thou? How does it feel to practice looking again, and yet again, and gaining greater respect for the uniqueness and immeasurability of the people across from me? What doors of perception open in these micro-moments of welcoming the More of who and what people actually are?

And as the other person enlarges toward their Thou-ness in my vision, can I too sink into more of my own Thou-ness? Can I learn to welcome this subtle opportunity? What if my various smaller parts agree to stand back and take it easy, as I let my internal boundaries expand out into my Thou-ness? How fine and freeing can this feel, even if for only a fraction of a second for now?

10. Gordon, *Tuning-In*, 80–82.

3

Our Dialogue Model: *WEG-VIBES*

HOW DO WE GET to where we're connecting, feeling, thinking, and inquiring together *with* others, and not merely settling for *talking at* one another? How do we get beyond trying to convince the other person we're right and they're not, which usually doesn't work anyway? Thomas Jefferson long ago observed that across the huge number of verbal arguments he'd witnessed in his lifetime,[1] he'd never seen, not even a single time, one disputant actually turning to the other and declaring, "You know what? It's clear to me now: you're right, and I'm wrong."

Let's face it, more often than we'd prefer, verbal debates can be a waste of time and energy, as well as spawn costly collateral damage. As an alternative we can choose to proceed in the way of dialogue.

In addition to viewing other people with eyes of *I-Thou* rather than *I-It*, what else do we need to put into practice in order to get past impersonal back-and-forth disputes and experience the taste of actual *shared inquiry*? If we want to use our minds more freshly *with* others, whether to have deep meaningful conversations or just for the fun of it in lighter conversation, how else do we also begin, what are the keys to dialoguing?

Our working answer: the time-tested **WEG-VIBES** dialogue model. The model consists of eight core practices: *Warmth, Empathy, Genuineness, Vulnerability, Imagination and Improvisation, Being Now and Here, Equality of Participation*, and *Suspending*. These have long been recognized within the dialogue literature as being practices of central importance.[2] A "practice" is an activity regularly pursued to bring a desired outcome into existence, and the eight **WEG-VIBES** practices are what it takes to get us to *person-centered* dialoguing.

1. Isaacs, *Dialogue*, 17.
2. Cissna and Anderson, "Ground of Dialogue," 9–33.

Let's begin our move through our **WEG-VIBES** practices by again citing the approach of Carl Rogers, a major figure in the study of dialogue.[3]

Warmth, Empathy, Genuineness. Safe and nurturing conversational containers begin with *Warmth* (e.g., Caring, Accepting, Respecting, Prizing), *Empathy* (heart-felt and mind-felt understanding), and *Genuineness* (authenticity, honesty, sincerity, realness). These are at the heart of the *person-centered* approach.

To attain open-ended personal dialogue, we need a communication climate filled with *Warmth*, *Empathy*, and *Genuineness*. The theorizing and research of eminent twentieth century psychologist Dr. Carl Rogers revolved around identifying, studying, and applying these three core practices.[4] They're at the center of creating higher quality communication climates and building healthy containers for dialoguing.

The presence of W-E-G provides a supportive environment that feels comforting, safe, and non-threatening. To bring personal dialogue into being we start with W-E-G, and refresh W-E-G throughout. Safety is needed for sound footing in dialogue, and we can best establish felt-safety by forging a secure dialogue container made of *Warmth*, *Empathy*, and *Genuineness*. Absent *Warmth*, *Empathy*, and *Genuineness* the probability of authentic dialogue occurring takes a dramatic nosedive.

These three core communication climate conditions, W-E-G, are valuable in *any* type of communication context, even during small talk and casual social conversation.[5] To create open-ended *person-centered* dialoguing, however, they become especially important.

Yet these three *W-E-G* practices combined, and the *I-Thou* atmosphere they so directly contribute to, are not our complete dialogue package. There are five additional practices that also matter if our dialoguing is to blossom, and I call these the **VIBES** practices. Our three **W-E-G** practices and our other five practices add up to **WEG-VIBES** (rhymes with Peg-Vibes), and an easy way to remember these eight core dialogue practices is with this mnemonic device.

These **WEG-VIBES** practices are game-changing superpowers, the heavy-duty real deal. In tandem they can up-level conversation to the dialogical realm. These eight primary dialogue practices are interdependent

3. Cissna and Anderson, "Contributions of Carl Rogers," 125–47.

4. Rogers, *Carl Rogers Reader*, Ch. 8, 10, 16, 17, 27. 29–32; see also Rogers, "Basic Conditions."

5. Gordon, *Tuning-In*, 35–46.

and interwoven, yet each highlights a particular facet of the process of bringing dialogical moments into being.

We'll briefly overview the **VIBES** practices now to give their flavor then further develop each of our **WEG-VIBES** practices in the chapters to follow.

Vulnerability. In exploratory dialogue we practice making ourselves more *Vulnerable*, we say things that are not rehearsed, not perfectly worded, not 100 percent risk-free. We choose to approach the edge of our comfort zone, we venture outside our cocoon. We practice becoming bold enough to risk *Vulnerability*, to at times risk having our mouths moving ahead of our minds, to risk looking silly, or weak, or soft, or some other way that part of us doesn't want to appear. We go past letting concern with appearances stop us, past allowing our small ego-self to hold us back, and instead boldly step into *Vulnerability*,

And for highly *generative* dialoguing to happen, where we're hoping to emerge with especially innovative thinking, we very much need to be willing to leap into the vast mental unknown, to seize moments and take risks without guarantees. We soften our self-consciousness and our protective outer-layering and practice surprising ourselves. We willingly allow our mask to crack, and ideally lay it down. We do this to become *more* than we typically dare let ourselves be. This is the stuff of *Vulnerability* and dialoguing.

We can best invite and welcome *Vulnerability*, of course, when all of us together are filling our dialogical container with *Warmth*, *Empathy*, and *Genuineness*. Our felt-safety is what lubricates the way for *Vulnerability*.

Imagination and Improvisation. Directly related to *Vulnerability*, for maximally exciting and creative dialoguing to emerge, when this be our desire, we'll want to practice *Imagination and Improvisation*. We call upon the muse of *Imagination* and become public dreamers with our thinking, words, and visions. We experiment with taking a break from unrelenting rationality and spontaneously imagine our way past fixed categories, labels, and patterns. Enough of boring order, we take comfort in launching into refreshing shades of creative chaos together.

We mind-play, mixing and matching our words, becoming expressive, colorful, light, and carefree. In highly *generative* dialoguing where we're aiming for a free-flow of creative images and ideas we have fun letting our imaginations run and play child-like. Humor can be of great value here for humor often deals with unpredictability, violated expectations, incongruity of imagery, and toying around. Humor and playfulness can unlock innovation, and in dialoguing we come to know and trust this.

We benefit from the courage to make ourselves *Vulnerable,* to risk playing at our edges in the service of the greater good. *Vulnerability* and *Imagination and Improvisation* work hand in hand to catalyze our most creative dialoguing, resting within the supportive embrace of *W-E-G,* our underlying foundational source of safety and strength.

Being Now and Here. In dialoguing we practice going beyond thinking mostly about the past and what once was, or ruminating upon the future and what might yet come. When overdone these can be distracting and draining mental pastimes. When it's time for dialoguing we practice opening ourselves to *present-centeredness,* our awareness being right here where our body is in space and time, less split and fragmented, more wholly *Here* and *Now.*

We breathe in and out as we *Slow Down*; and then again in, and out, as we *Stand Back*; and then we breathe in another breath as we start to *See More,* and then we breathe out; and then we *Step Forth Wisely* by breathing and centering ourselves into scintillating aliveness in this leading-edge moment. Let's do this now, if we haven't already, transcending *Then-mind* and *There-mind* and becoming more compellingly *Now* and *Here* as we follow our tool of choice, our breathing. With *present-centeredness* our consciousness is better positioned to surge into multi-directional functionality, leveraging us so we can shoot through portals of deeper insight and voicing from within the fertile potentiality of *Now-Being.*

Yet even when we're not out for highly creative dialoguing and simply want to enjoy a milder conversation together our *present-centeredness* serves purpose, communicating to our dialogue partners that we're not distracted by our own *Then* and *There.* It communicates that we *care,* that we want to be giving priority and respect to our conversational partners and to our dialoguing. This in turn promotes trust.

Research shows that people are mentally present only about half the time they're supposedly "listening" to others. In dialoguing we seek to change this by sensing from within ourselves how it actually *feels* for us to bodily be more *present.* Inhabiting our body with greater awareness is our way out of our head and back to *Now.* And our breathing process specifically is one of our primary bodily pathways for returning to *Now* and *Here* present-centeredness.

This answer is so simple, and right under our nose. Totally portable, wherever we go, it's always with us, so very close, right here, a breath away. All we need to do is slow down and become aware: *Here, Now.* This will be among our ongoing practices.

Equality of Participation. Whether two of us or twenty of us are engaging in dialoguing, we want to correct any imbalances in participation. If anyone tries to *dominate* dialogue they'll in fact *block* dialogue. Acting from egoism is a barrier to dialogue. Everyone needs equal opportunity and encouragement to enter dialogue so that our conversation can be free of power hierarchies and conversational narcissism. Every person's voice is vital to squeezing the most out of the dialogue, and in dialogue we continue to remember and repeatedly act upon this fact. Dialogue is authentically democratic: anything other, interesting though it may be, is not full dialogue.

As an analogy, we benefit from all twenty-six letters of the English alphabet: consistently take away the "n," subtract the "d," get rid of the "t," remove the "a," and do the same for a few more letters, and our discourse ultimately suffers. Just as each letter (or emoji) serves its important role, each person has their unique voice to bring to our dialoguing, their piece of the puzzle. We practice returning to this essential recognition and acting upon it. Fair distribution among voices in *person-centered* dialogue needs to be generously sought and protected.

Suspending. Dr. David Bohm, one of the twentieth century's leading dialogue theorists, once surmised that some "scientists" might be among the toughest candidates for reaching true dialogue since so many scientists are intellectually wedded to their own schools of thought, paradigms, pet theories about what's true and what's not, and skeptical of alternative possibilities.[6]

To get to free-flowing dialoguing, however, we need to repeatedly practice more *lightly holding* our ideas, positions, judgments, images, and opinions. Instead of tightly clutching each belief and thought and label that's passing through our mind, during dialoguing we actively practice *softening our mental grip.* We practice dis-identifying with these passing contents of consciousness, becoming more fluid within our mind so that our thinking can more dynamically flow.[7]

---

6. Bohm, *On Creativity*, 139–40.
7. Bohm, *On Dialogue*, Ch. 6.

We deepen our willingness to *Suspend,* to temporarily ease-off our mental and emotional attachments to what we think we know and feel. We practice awakening spaciousness within our mind for new images, ideas, and thinking to arrive and thrive. *Suspending* makes space for liquidity of thought flow. We stop internally and externally defending prior positions. We lighten it up, since dialoguing is not about defense and counter-attack of positions but instead about *joint inquiry.* We remember we're standing side-by-side, surveying the landscape together with our dialogue partners, and less intensely holding on to the contents of our individual minds. We choose to temporarily *Suspend.*

In sum, with the acronym *WEG-VIBES* we have a succinct handle on the fundamental practices for bringing *person-centered* dialogue into being: *Warmth, Empathy, and Genuineness; Vulnerability; Imagination and Improvisation; Being Now and Here; Equality of Participation;* and *Suspending.* We practice *WEG-VIBES* with calm mind and body as we center and ground ourselves in the present moment, relatively unified in our being.

To become aware of the right timing for each of these practices during a conversation we remember and *feel* our breathing, as we *Slow Down (inhale, exhale); Stand Back (inhale, exhale); See More (inhale, exhale);* and eventually *Step Forth Wisely (inhale, exhale).* It's worth our while to do this, for we're planting healthy seeds in our mind, body, and being.

These then are our cardinal practices for giving birth to dialogue. Minus these chief practices, or, worse yet, with their opposites prevailing, it's difficult for dialoguing to flower. As communication scholar Dr. Bud Goodall once said, "Dialogue challenges us to swim with the flow of the talk and trust the fluid context and fluid boundaries of self and other to support a particular type of talk, more fluid and boundary-less . . . "[8] To have our conversation become this smooth and liquid we need to be awash in *WEG-VIBES.* They are the waters in which we float.

Much as we would tune a musical instrument to have its sounds smoothly flow, we tune ourselves for *person-centered* dialoguing as we ease into *WEG-VIBES,* and as we relax into our bodies, our breathing, and our hearts. *WEG-VIBES* can permit us to reach advanced levels of feeling, thinking, and becoming curious together.

Advocacy aside for now, we learn what it means to truly *inquire together.* No winners, no losers, no one up, no one down. We ease off our solitary certitude and become co-travelers, proclaiming less and wondering

8. Goodall, Jr. and Kellett, "Pathways to Peak Experiences," 169.

more. We allow our edges to become permeable by softening them in our mind's eye, and by ever so slightly relaxing our physical structure. We invite our senses to awaken, our hearts to open, and our mind to enlarge.

When we're with one or more people and feel dialoguing could be useful we remember **WEG-VIBES**. We use this as our checklist to measure how we're doing with one another in these vital areas and as a roadmap for moving forward. As we make these core practices for dialogue explicitly known to the people with whom we're wanting to be dialoguing we increase the odds of our conversation getting off the ground, taking flight, and uplifting into dialogue. This becomes a self-fulfilling prophecy: our expectations affect our actions, and our actions influence our outcomes.

Dr. Robert Hutchins said in the mid-twentieth century that "The Civilization of the Dialogue is the only civilization worth having, and the only civilization in which the whole world can unite. It is, therefore, the only civilization we can hope for, because the world must unite or be blown to bits."[9] Competence in the practices of human dialogue in the remainder of this twenty-first century is more essential than ever before all across our planet.

We can begin in our small way to enact a local civilization of *person-centered* dialoguing in our own location and on our own topics. These topics don't have to be earth shaking, or ripped from today's headlines. In fact, let's not start there, instead let's talk about things that are meaningful to us but that are not quick to elicit polarization of belief. We want to give ourselves ample opportunity to practice *person-centered* dialogue successfully. We can move on to more controversial and divisive topics down the road if we so choose, but for now let's be good to ourselves and our education in the way of dialoguing.

So what again is dialogue?

I choose to define *dialogue* "operationally": that is, to the extent that we're enacting our **WEG-VIBES** practices as we engage in *shared inquiry* with one another, we're practicing *person-centered* dialogue. As we perform these operations, we're doing what we need to. On the *monologue-to-dialogue* continuum, as we activate **WEG-VIBES** we're no longer at the impersonal *monologue* end of the continuum, we're up within the *dialogue* zone of this spectrum.

In other words, we can best respond to the question "Are we doing dialogue yet?" by asking, "Are we doing **WEG-VIBES** yet?" And the more skilled

9. See Matson and Montagu, *Human Dialogue*, vi.

and nuanced we become at our practice of **WEG-VIBES** as we undertake *shared inquiry* together, the higher the quality of our dialoguing.

Person-centered dialoguing, then, is an alternative to the nasty-spirited and polarizing communication styles prevalent all around us today. By using **WEG-VIBES** as we delve into thinking and feeling together with others, we remind ourselves and one another of our common humanity. This reminder is no small accomplishment, and we gladly start here.

Today's generation is the first-ever to have electronic communication tools in place that can now allow the human species to think, feel, and act effectively together for the future well-being of humankind and all other life forms on our planet. *Person-centered* face-to-face and electronic dialoguing has to begin in earnest somewhere; may it begin with us, and grow from the sorts of initial undertakings recommended in this volume. May it eventually, when more people are ready and capable, come to include topics that are even more challenging. But we start from where we are, beginning to build bridges between us.

In our next readings we'll examine each of our eight core **WEG-VIBES** practices more intimately.

Taking Action

Learn what **WEG-VIBES** stands for. Memorize our set of eight core practices, get a handle on our working model so it becomes a roadmap in your mind, a template for action. Get a feel for the content of our model as you read on. Know that as you enthusiastically undertake these practices when you seek to *inquire together* with others you're bringing dialoguing into being.

Reflecting

Am I starting to notice when various of the WEG-VIBES conditions do and don't exist in conversations all around me, and in my own? What am I noticing about how WEG-VIBES opens dialogic spaces, and how their relative absence, or their opposites, narrow such spaces? May insights begin, and may I take them into my mind and bodily being.

4

Core Communication Practices: *W-E-G*

THE *I-THOU* MINDSET THAT Martin Buber so poetically writes about dovetails nicely with Dr. Carl Rogers' three major *person-centered* communication practices. A good way to shift into the *I-Thou* region of the *I-It* to *I-Thou* continuum is to treat our conversational partners with *Warmth*, *Empathy*, and *Genuineness (W-E-G)*. Focusing on these three interwoven person-centered core practices naturally primes us to view the other less as an *It* and more as *Thou*.

In the three readings to follow we'll examine *Warmth* and *Empathy* and *Genuineness* each in their turn. But I so greatly value *W-E-G* in providing us a solid container for dialogue that I want to yet again provide a quick panoramic view of them as an integrated set before then treating them one-by-one.

Who was Carl Rogers? Dr. Carl R. Rogers was ranked (using evidence-based criteria) as being among the top half-dozen "most eminent" twentieth century contributors to the academic discipline of psychology.[1] Dr. Rogers also received both the Distinguished Scientific Contribution Award and the Professional Contribution Award from the American Psychological Association, and served as President of the American Psychological Association. Just prior to his death he was nominated for the Nobel Peace Prize. Dr. Rogers was about as honored as a professional can be in the field of psychology, and his legacy continues to impact the world to this day.[2]

Looking back near the end of his career Dr. Rogers said that "caring about communication" was the "one overriding theme" of his entire professional life. He referred to his continuing interest in the topic as an "obsession with communication."[3] Since communication is so basic to

1. Haggbloom, "100 Most Eminent Psychologists," 139–52.
2. Barfield, "Evolution of Person-Centered Encounter."
3. Rogers, *A Way of Being*, 64–66.

human relationship he wanted to find the underlying laws of constructive human communication: what needs to be present for communication to be productive and satisfying?

Dr. Rogers and his doctoral students at Ohio State, the University of Chicago, and the University of Wisconsin conducted research into the core communication climate of growth-enhancing relationships. Dr. Rogers was the pioneer researcher in electronically recording counseling interviews. He and his research teams analyzed these interviews to discover those communication practices that fostered forward movement, discovery, and satisfaction, and those communication practices that did not.[4]

Ultimately three core communication practices were found to be of elemental importance in creating a constructive communication climate. These practices Dr. Rogers formally termed "*Unconditional Positive Regard,*" "*Empathy,*" and "*Congruence.*" More popularly he referred to these as *Warmth, Empathy,* and *Genuineness (W-E-G).*[5] In these pages I might at times refer to these as the Big 3 (though Dr. Rogers himself never referred to them this way, but usually as "the core conditions").

When these *W-E-G* attitudes and behaviors are present a communication climate is born that allows incredible things to happen within it. On the other hand, when the Big 3 are only minimally present, or even worse if their opposites are present (e.g., coldness, judgment, and insincerity), communication and relationship will be impeded, and possibly fail.

The Big 3 go right to the crux of spanning communication gaps and building bonds of communication and dialogue. They can enhance interpersonal attunement and communication satisfaction in all forms of human relationship. Dr. Rogers came to eventually hypothesize that *Warmth, Empathy, and Genuineness* are *trans-contextual,* that wherever people are trying to communicate in any personal or professional setting or circumstance, the presence or absence of *W-E-G* matters. For a half-century now, the Big 3 have been prominently positioned within the academic study of human dialogue.[6]

When the Big 3 operate in close conjunction with one another they form a robust and pliable structure. When well-integrated they can work

---

4. Rogers and Russell, *Quiet Revolutionary,* 130–34.

5. Rogers, *A Way of Being,* Ch.1,6,7; also see Rogers, "Basic Conditions."

6. Johannesen, "Communication as Dialogue," 373–82; Poulakos, "Components of Dialogue," 199–212' Stewart, "Foundations of Dialogic Communication," 183–201; Cissna and Anderson, "Contributions of Carl Rogers," 125–47.

wonders, each fortified by the others. Think of *W-E-G* as a triad, a triangle, a pyramid, an interconnected system. You know how when you interlace the fingers of your two hands together they smoothly fit? That's how the combination of *W-E-G* will feel when smoothly intertwined, and the *whole* becomes greater than any single one, or even all, of its parts.

Or maybe think of it this way: in the same way that a room has three major dimensions (length, width, and height) we can hold *Warmth*, *Empathy*, and *Genuineness* as our three-dimensional model for creating healthy dialogical containers with others, and with ourselves. The Big 3 practices yield a secure environment, a congenial vessel, a safe container, in which our communication and dialoguing can take shape. *W-E-G* provide us with comfort, safety, authenticity, possibility.

No safe container = no dialogue.

Warmth, *Empathy*, and *Genuineness* are foundational to a safe container.

The theory of the Big 3 has tremendous reach and parsimony, it's both strong and simple. Dr. Carl Rogers' *person-centered* approach will echo across these pages. We can ask ourselves at moments during conversation, "Right now, how much *Warmth* am I giving to this other person?" We can ask, "How much *Empathy*, from my head and heart, am I experiencing and communicating to this other person?" We can ask, "How *Genuine*, how sincere, real, and honestly self-disclosing am I being with this other person?" Dr. Rogers' theory of constructive communication environments possesses gold-standard simplicity and power. It provides us with guidance on what to aim toward as our conversational attempts at dialogue proceed.

When we combine the *person-centered approach* of Dr. Rogers with the *I-Thou* mindset that Dr. Martin Buber encourages, we have the makings of a fine atmosphere for open-ended dialoguing, one in which people can begin to feel safe and secure, and this is essential for dialogue to take root and flourish. We breathe in, and breathe out, as we *Slow Down*; we take another slow breath in and out as we *Stand Back*; we breathe in deeply again, as we move into *Seeing More*; and then in and out once more, as we ultimately proceed to *Step Forth Wisely*.

Whenever I use the word "dialogue" in these pages, know that I'm using it as a shorthand term for the lengthier expression *person-centered* dialogue as embedded in the work of Drs. Rogers and Buber. We keep our eye not on *positions*, but on mutually sustaining our *personhood* as we *inquire together*. There is a distinct "turning toward" our dialogical partners, and this we recognize and feel.

In the next three readings we'll look more closely at the core *person-centered* practices of *Warmth, Empathy, and Genuineness* each in turn. Then we'll consider the five additional practices that are also vital components of the human dialogue process.

Taking Action

Start to watch and listen to yourself as you have conversations with others. Ask yourself whether you think you're low, medium, high, or somewhere in-between on each of the Big 3. At the end of the day, ask which of the Big 3 has been your strongest suit that day, and which your weakest. Memorize the Big 3, and begin to be on the lookout for them, especially when you want your conversations to be less about trading monologues and more about *thinking together* with someone else. Start to observe yourself in action and ask: "What am I doing here right now in terms of *W-E-G*?" Mindful self-awareness is our leverage point, our powerful entry place.

Reflecting

What happens as I watch my behavior as I talk with other people this week, as I look down from the ceiling and see and hear how Warm, Empathic, and Genuine I'm being?

And what if all along the way I decide to give to myself what I intend to give others: Warmth, Empathy, and Genuineness? Am I able to trust that my own personal development will come more through self-directed W-E-G than from self-criticism?

Can I be a good friend to myself as I at the same time upgrade my conversational relations with others? Can I open to my Thou dimension, and be receptive to healthy W-E-G radiating from this dimension of my being and filling up my parts with love, understanding, and honesty?

5

The Practice of Warmth

UNCONDITIONAL POSITIVE REGARD, ALSO known as *Warmth*, has to do with allowing the other person to feel *deeply "Cared About," "Accepted," "Respected," "Prized," "Valued," "Appreciated,"* and *"Loved."* Read these terms again, slowly. Get a feeling for *Warmth* and what it conveys as Dr. Rogers conceptualized it. In my communication classes I have students learn the acronym *CARP* to mentally retrieve the elements of *Caring, Accepting, Respecting,* and *Prizing,* each of which was of stand-out importance to Dr. Rogers when talking about *Warmth*.

My own favorite term from among these four main aspects of the *Warmth* component is *Prizing*. Have you ever been treated by someone as though you were *valuable* and *precious* to them, as though you were truly *prized*? It's a great feeling, and encourages us to feel good both about ourselves and the other person. It also sets the stage for further personal unfoldment.

In Hawai'i where I live and work the commonly used word *Aloha* means much of what Dr. Rogers means by *Warmth,* or *Unconditional Positive Regard. Aloha* is an unconditional loving acceptance of the other person graciously extended from the heart and directed to the heart of the other person.

Like the spirit of *Aloha,* Dr. Rogers' *Warmth* is not a mental phenomenon, a logic-based cognitive construct, it's more of a kind and embracing *feeling* that radiates from one person to another and surrounds both. It creates an interpersonal ambiance that can be palpable and potent. We warm the heart of the other person with our own *Warmth*.

For Dr. Rogers *Warmth* is unconditional, meaning that the other person does not have to earn it, we simply extend it to them because of their intrinsic worth as a living being. They are granted our *Warmth,* our *Unconditional Positive Regard* because of their intrinsic humanity.

This does not mean we would necessarily agree with everything this other person might think or say or do in this world. It's not an endorsement of all their beliefs and actions. But it does mean that we hold an underlying respect for their personhood, their status as a human being, and their potential for even further actualizing beyond where they are now.

Warmth gets communicated in part through our words. To have another feel our *Warmth* for them, we share our kind words with them. We make statements that are appreciative, accepting, supportive, positive, friendly, praiseful, encouraging, uplifting, and loving. We might say "I'm eager to hear whatever you might have to say here, I so much respect how your mind works," or "That was very thoughtful of you to let me get all that out, I really thank you!" or "I appreciate your insight in what you just shared," or "I love talking with you, you're very open-minded and receptive," or "That's one of the many things I've always admired about you, your words are colorful and alive," or "You never interrupt me, and I want you to know I value you for being generous to me in this way." These sorts of verbal strokes, when sincerely meant, feel good to receive; we bask in them, like reclining into a warm bath.

Warmth is also communicated through our nonverbal behaviors: our supportive tone of voice, our kind face, our friendly smile, our warm eyes, our open and receptive posture, our reassuring physical closeness to the other, our gentle and loving touch, and our generous actions. All these nonverbal channels when used well can communicate our *Warmth* to another person. Sometimes these nonverbal messages accompany warm words, and other times they stand on their own.

Warmth flows especially heavily through the nonverbal channels. In a classic University of Massachusetts study it was found that *nonverbal behaviors were five times more important than words in communicating Warmth!*[1] What we do with our facial expressions of caring involvement, our supportive head nodding, our sincere smiling, our congenial eye contact, our turning toward the other person and not away from them, our kind voice, this is where much of the action is in the practice of *Warmth*.

We become more aware of our bodies and what someone could see us as saying through them. We self-monitor what we might be giving-off. We become increasingly aware not only of the words leaving our mouth but also of what our body and vocal intonations could be communicating. Developing

---

1. Tepper and Haase, "Nonverbal Facilitative Conditions," 200–04.

this self-awareness, this mindfulness, is part of our practice of *Warmth*. We Slow Down, Stand Back, See More, and then Step Forth Wisely.

We come to know that "we cannot *not* behave." We realize that we're constantly emitting behaviors, and that any of these behaviors can be interpreted by others as *messages* to them about them, even when that's not what we're intending. We practice seeing and hearing what we're doing at any given moment on this fundamentally important dimension that runs from *Coldness* to *Warmth*.

When people feel human *Warmth* directed at them through nonverbal and verbal channels of communication they tend to light-up with contentment, as compared to how bad they feel when faced with a communication climate of *Coldness* (*e.g.*, neutrality, non-caring, judgment, unfriendliness, maybe even dislike and hostility). *Warmth* communicates that the other person matters to us, that we want to be kind and supportive toward them, that we confirm them in their essential humanity. When people clearly receive such warm heart-to-heart messages they glow, and then they grow. Dr. Rogers concluded that it activates the *actualizing tendency*, the person's innate potential for further growth and development.[2]

At times, of course, it helps to *Slow Down* and smile as we breathe in and out; and then to *Stand Back* inside ourselves as we breathe our way into our own easygoing *Warmth*; and then we breathe in and out again as we *See More* of the *Warmth* that we have within ourselves to give; and then we breathe in and out once more as we *Step Forth Warmly* out into our world. We periodically return to relaxing into our breathing, and into our heart of *Warmth*.

Time and time again the practice of *Warmth* in human interaction has been shown to have major impact, both under scientific laboratory conditions and in the world of everyday communication. For more than seven decades we've scientifically known that the *Warmth-Coldness* dimension is of central importance in how we Americans perceive other people: we're eager to interact with others we see as being *Warm*, but not so drawn to people we perceive as *Cold*.[3]

Yet it's not only in the America where perceptions of *Warmth* matter. Dr. Amy Cuddy of Harvard University and her colleagues recently found in the nearly two-dozen countries they studied that the very first quality

2. Rogers, *A Way of Being*, 117–26.
3. Asch, "Forming Impressions of Personality."

people tend to look for in another person, all around the world, is how much *Warmth* or *Coldness* they're seen as displaying.[4]

With *Coldness* facing them people remain leery, suspicious, and on guard. They tend to want to *Move Away* from or *Move Against* another person perceived as *Cold*. This is part of an ancient mindset, part of our built-in cautiousness, a survival strategy that served our ancestors well in keeping them alive. People much prefer to see *Warmth*, for in the presence of *Warmth* we can feel safer and calm down, we can relax, we feel we can better trust the other.[5]

My friend Bryan was recently telling me about a particularly glum and uninspired day he was having, but when he all of a sudden saw a brightly smiling face looking squarely at and into him, it changed his inner and outer worlds for rest of his day. Weeks later he still recalls that transformative smile with joy and delight. He lights up telling this story, the *Warmth* still lingering strongly.

Warmth uplifts and sustains us, *Warmth* connects us, *Warmth* repairs and heals us. *Warmth* is a force for the Good.

Dr. Rogers didn't invent *Warmth*, of course, it has existed for thousands of years in the hearts of people in cultures all across the globe. What he did do was to empirically verify that when we want to create a constructive and growth-promoting communication climate, then *Warmth* (including *Caring, Accepting, Respecting, Prizing*) matters.

For dialoguing especially, *Warmth* is a central requirement. In order for dialogue to arise and energize, people need to feel comfortable and secure enough with one another to venture into often uncharted realms together. This can occur as our dialogue container is filled with *Warmth*.

In the same way that the sun is at the heart of our galaxy, our beating heart inside of us is our own personal sun, and with our inner sun we can shine our *Warmth* onto and into those who come within our orbit. When dialoguing partners are shining their sun-bright *Warmth* upon and into one another, intimacy and unfoldment spring alive.

When Martin Buber sat in weekly personal dialogues with his young friend and student Aubrey Hodes (fifty years Buber's junior), Buber's non-verbal *Warmth* behaviors were described by Hodes this way: "When he said something he leaned back in his chair, relaxed, coming straight to the focal point of his idea. But when I replied or suggested some new idea he moved

4. Cuddy, *Presence*, Ch. 3.
5. Porges, *Polyvagal Theory*, Ch. 3.

32

forward in his chair, concentrated on every syllable, encouraging me with his eyes, those wonderful eyes which were so penetrating, piercing, yet so warm, friendly and good . . . Buber's face, so alert and receptive, so rock-fast and free, so open to the presence of his companions."[6] This is *Warmth*, the outward shine of Buber's sun, and Hodes basked in its rays and sprang to life, his insights and ideas and questions flowed.

Carl Rogers, too, emanated the *Unconditional Positive Regard*, the *Warmth*, of which he spoke and wrote. I remember once attending a lecture by the world famous behaviorist psychologist B.F. Skinner and roughly a quarter of the audience left the university gym before the talk was finished, maybe because the lecture was rather impersonal and *Cold*. Months later I attended a public talk by Dr. Rogers, and at the end of his talk 3,000 people stood in standing ovation, in large part, I believe, because Dr. Rogers had touched our hearts with his *Warmth*, his *Empathy*, and his *Genuineness*. He practiced what he taught: his authentic *Warmth* and humanity brightly shined on us all.

Warmth not only confirms us in our being and make us feel good, it also opens us up and allows our creative thinking to stream more freely. In a *generative* dialogue group where we're especially searching out innovative ideas and angles of approach, *Unconditional Positive Regard* fosters our productivity. One meta-analysis of over a hundred separate scientific studies on "ideational fluency" (quantity of production of ideas, images, and associations) clearly showed that "positive mood" enhances creative thinking, while states such as "fear" and "anxiety" decrease creativity.[7] We know from our own experience that *Coldness* does not encourage a positive mood. It is *Warmth* that builds and broadens our mental expansiveness, and our interpersonal relationships.

When you want to have an open-ended collaborative dialogue with others, *Warmth* is a prerequisite. Model *Warmth* yourself, and if you're in a dialogue group talk publicly with the other participants about the utter importance of verbal and nonverbal *Warmth* in establishing and maintaining a comfortable, safe, secure, fun climate in which the sharing of personal insights and discoveries can prosper.

When *Warmth* wanes, dialogue dribbles.

6. Hodes, *Encounter with Martin Buber*, 24.
7. Baas, "Meta-Analysis of Mood–Creativity Research," 779–806.

THE WAY OF DIALOGUE

We repeatedly recycle through our human need for *Warmth*. It's not a one-and-done. We all recurrently return to wanting to have the sunshine of *Warmth* glowing upon us.

And everyone, and everything, grows as *Warmth* shines its rays.

We need to understand and practice exactly this in our dialogical conversations: we benefit in multiple ways from endlessly returning to the "positivity resonance" that the atmospheric field of *Unconditional Positive Regard* stimulates.

Taking Action

Start to become aware of your own verbal and nonverbal cues of *Warmth* during your conversations. What do you see and hear? When you find yourself on the colder side, slip into releasing more *Warmth*. Find yourself saying some kind, nice, encouraging, reinforcing, sweet, supportive, and appreciative words, more than usual, and see what happens.

Take yourself off-guard at moments, set aside any miserly habits and dare to release your goodwill, your *Warmth* toward the other person or what they've said, and your good feelings about being with them. Brush away the clouds, let your sun shine right through your words and face and tone of voice, warming-up your heart and theirs.

Focus on all the areas of *SOFTEN*: *Smiling, Open body language, Facial supportiveness, Forward motion, Tone of supportiveness, Touch of support, Eye contact to support, and Nodding to show support*. These are the key non-verbal zones where the communication of *Warmth* is located.[8] Allow your nonverbal actions here to work not *against* you and others, but rather *for* the good of the whole.

Pick one or two of these NV behaviors at a time and become mindfully aware of what you're doing in these couple of areas while interacting with others. Then pick another one or two. Rotate around, and stay with it. Warm-up your nonverbal communication. People feel safer and more comfortable with you when they *feel* your *Warmth* emanating from you, and from all of those who are part of the dialogue. *Coldness* kills, while *Warmth* restores and sustains life. This healing *Warmth* travels mightily through the nonverbal channels of communication, as well as through our words.

---

8. Gordon, *Tuning-In*, 71–76.

Reflecting

Since Warmth vs. Coldness is of ultimate importance in building a solid container for communication and dialogue, what do I learn about Warmth and Coldness by watching and hearing other people throughout my day? Do I notice how Coldness "kills"? And how Warmth brings life to life?

And how is Warmth being shown (or not) through my own nonverbal communication in any given conversation? And through my words? When I and others create an atmosphere of Warmth, how does this look and feel? In this practice area am I becoming aware of my breathing as I Slow Down? And also as I choose to Stand Back? And am I feeling my body breathing in and out as I come to See More? And am I breathing deeply yet quietly, in through my nostrils, and out through my mouth, as I glide into Stepping Forth Wisely with Warmth?

Am I welcoming my heart to calm down, and melt its emotional essence into soothing shades of lovingkindness? Can I open my mind to increasingly feeling lovingkindness as it courses through me, and as it's communicating my Warmth to others? What might this be like if I could sense such a flow of lovingkindness, even if for only a fraction of a second? Is it conceivable that I can know this?

6

The Practice of Empathy

EMPATHY, THE SECOND OF Dr. Rogers' core facilitative conditions, involves communicating to the other person that we deeply understand, with both our head and our heart, what they're trying to communicate to us. Not only do we understand the *surface meanings* of their words, but we're also grasping underlying *personal meanings* and deeper *feelings* that exist behind and beneath their words.[1]

Empathy is a *person-centered* way of listening. With *Empathy* we're able to *de-center* from our own personal point of view, and *re-center* within the perceptual world of the other person. We become at home in their inner world, and move delicately there. We come to understand how their world might look and feel to them from *their* vantage point. This is the work of *Empathy*. When human beings attempt to create dialogue, the presence or absence of *Mutual Empathy* matters, and will affect outcomes.

Mutual Empathy is an extraordinary gateway to abundance.

Dr. Rogers noted that "Every individual exists in a continually changing world of experience of which s/he is the center. The organism reacts to the field as it is experienced and perceived. The perceptual field is, for the individual, 'reality.'"[2] With *Empathy* we're able to extend past our own personal borders and get closer to the other person's "reality" as they know and experience it. We become more attuned to what the other is thinking and feeling, and why.

We attempt to look through *their eyes* at their world, and have the other person *feel* us doing this. For someone to *feel* empathically understood by us, both our words and nonverbal behaviors need to resonate with what they're going through. We become their "confident companion" in

1. Rogers, *A Way of Being*, Ch. 7.
2. Rogers, *A Way of Being*, Ch. 5.

this moment, as Dr. Rogers liked to put it. *Empathy* dissolves alienation, it confirms a person's existence and humanity.

It's an accomplishment when mutual understanding is brought into being, when all participants in a conversation or dialogue feel *mutually empathically understood* by one another. I once did a small study of mutual understanding where over a hundred participants were given a Columbia University research instrument of nearly 400 items, and each person privately selected those descriptive statements that, for them, best captured the condition of high mutual understanding.[3]

The bottom-line: when people believe that a high degree of *mutual understanding* has been created they feel *Comforted, Awakened, Moving Toward & With the Other,* and *Empowered.* The single item most frequently chosen to capture the experience of being in a state of high *mutual understanding* was this one: "*I'm optimistic and cheerful, the world seems basically beautiful, people are essentially kind, life is worth living, the future seems bright*" (chosen by over 75 percent of both females and males). Out of almost 400 items this single statement most captured the positive impact, the "goodness" resulting from people feeling *mutually understood* by one another.

In dialogue people want to feel that their dialogue partners care enough to pay attention to them and what they're saying. They want not a passive and neutral audience; they want their listener to *enter into* what they're trying to communicate, they want personal involvement and responsiveness. They want to *feel felt.* They want what they say and who they are to be notably acknowledged and respected. *Empathy* has been called "oxygen for the soul." This is the work of *Empathic* listening: to permit the other person to feel highly received, understood, and oxygenated, because we have listened to them with our "whole being."

The practice of *Empathy* involves both the head and the heart. We know there's something inside the other person they're at times groping to express accurately, and we want to help them achieve clarity and release. We *care* enough to want to know the subtle shadings of what they mean. We at times ask them *questions of clarification* aimed at probing the meanings behind their words: "What are you saying about . . .?" "When you use the expression 'too bold,' what are you meaning there?" "When you talked about it seeming 'unethical,' what were you suggesting?" "Do you mean . . .?" "Can you tell me

---

3. Gordon, *Tuning-In,* 60–65.

in different words what you're trying to get at here?" "Will you run that by me again, maybe with another example this time?"

All of these *questions of clarification* are intended to get *behind* words used and into the people using those words. This is motivated by kind-hearted curiosity. We care enough to want to sincerely understand what the other person is really *meaning*, and we know that peoples' *meanings* are more *inside* them than within the external words they use. We kindly probe, to take us yet closer.

We can also *paraphrase* the other person, translating back to them in our own words what we think they meant by their words. This can be a potent method of correcting our misunderstandings and getting us closer to someone's intended meaning. When our *paraphrase* feels spot-on to the other person then they know they're getting through to us. *Paraphrasing* is a marvelous communication tool that can help facilitate genuine dialogue, a tool that's vastly underused. When dialoguing we rely on *paraphrasing* now and again.

Again, in *paraphrasing* we're tentatively reflecting back, but in different words, what we hear our dialogue partner to be meaning. We might preface our *paraphrase* with words such as these: "I hear you saying . . ." "Here's what I think you're expressing . . ." "Let me tell you what I think you're meaning, and see if I've got it right . . ." "Can I summarize for you what I'm getting from what you're saying?" "I'd like to *paraphrase* for you what I'm taking away from what you've said . . ." "I'd like to *reflect back to you* what I'm receiving, to see if I'm understanding you correctly . . ."

In each case we go ahead and tell the other person in our words what we think they're perhaps trying to communicate to us. We're translating back to them our own tentative version of what we think they mean, to see how close to or far away from their *intended meaning* we are. This *paraphrasing (reflecting back)* assists us in narrowing communication gaps. We keep it exploratory in tone; we're inquiring, rather than declaring certitude, and our tentative tone of voice conveys this. We don't merely parrot back, instead we give our tentative translations.

We can eventually skip the prefacing and just tell the other person in our own words what we've gotten out of what they've said. Sometimes the prefaces slow us down and can even start to seem artificial with repetition, so we learn to more seamlessly cut to the chase over time. I paraphrase my wife many times a day, for example, and with that degree of frequency the prefaces would become excessive and sound gimmicky. No need, a tentative translation alone suffices.[4]

The knowledge we seek with our practice of *Empathy* is not head knowledge alone, of course, it's also heart knowledge. We not only want to see how our dialogue partner is intellectually seeing and thinking about things, but also reverberate with how they're emotionally *feeling* about these things. The word *Empathy* has both Greek and German roots and translates as *feeling into*.[5] As we set our intention on *Empathizing* we in essence choose to lay aside ourselves for now and *feel our way into* the meanings and experiencing of this other person. We become less preoccupied with what *we* think and feel and more focused on the other person and what *they* think and feel. We foray into our dialogue partner's inner world and gracefully move about.

One of the beneficial side effects of choosing to enter the realm of the other is that it gives us a nice time-out from our own self-preoccupations. We abandon our own concerns and anxieties, leaving them behind somewhat as we move toward becoming the other. We forget ourselves, even if incompletely so, and as one classic Zen statement puts it "To forget the self is to be one with others."[6]

So with *Empathy* we forge an interconnection with this other person resulting from our *I-Thou* envisioning, our caring *questions of clarification*, our periodic *paraphrasing*, and our opening into the *Warmth* and *Empathy* that resides within our human heart. With *Empathy* we hear not only what the other says to us but also, at moments, we even hear what they haven't yet said even to themselves. We have gotten closer, "as if" we are walking in their shoes.

This is not to say that accurate mutual understanding is always necessary throughout a dialogical conversation, because it's not. The late Dr. David Bohm, one of the twentieth century deans of dialogue, was quick to point out that miscommunication and misunderstanding can often be of value in *generative* dialogue when we're wanting to extremely innovative. We can use the *difference* between *intention* and *impact* to bring new creation into being.[7] We can hijack our misconstrued meanings and use them as fodder for generative play; we can alchemically transform our

---

4. Miller, *Listening Well*, Ch. 12.

5. Rifkin, *Empathic Civilization*, Ch. 1.

6. Herrigel, *Zen in the Art of Archery*, 47–61.

7. Bohm, *On Dialogue*, Ch. 1.

miscommunication into emergent delights. There are instances where our breakdowns can become breakouts, out of confinement and into avant-garde verbal inventiveness.

My friend Steve and I, for example, regularly play with language in our conversations, and we at times deliberately choose to playfully "mishear" one another so that we can then generatively play off of the uncertainties we create by intentionally *not* understanding the other person. So Steve says something about linguist Noam Chomsky and I'll respond with a statement about Nome, Alaska, and we're off and running. In generative conversation this wordplay can be hugely fun and rousingly innovative. We coin new terms, we play with puns, we kid around and get outlandish together, and we end up uttering things that have never been said before exactly like this on the planet Earth. What fun, and the piñata breaks.

Typically, however, *mutual understanding* is desirable in our daily communication, including within our dialogical conversations. *Empathy* is the route past mundane two-dimensional understanding and into three-dimensional resonance where we totally "get" the other person's meanings and our brain-firings become synchronized, we become brain-coupled.[8] When we understand one another we get brain-aligned, we are each tuned-in to the other. Through the practice of *Mutual Empathy*, people entering into the minds and hearts of one another, the flying "V" can stretch far <.

Dr. Bohm called dialogue a "superconductor" where ideas can at times coolly flow without friction. Being on the same wavelength with others in *Mutual Empathy* enables this *super-conductance*; and when this happens, we become cool and fly together.

Taking Action

How can we transition into *Empathy*? One way is to pause and reboot. As we take breath #1 slowly in, and then out, we remind ourselves that we're choosing to *Slow Down*. As we gently take our next inhalation and exhalation, breath #2, we become aware of our choice to *Stand Back*. With our third in-breath and out-breath we softly focus on *Seeing More*, realizing that maybe we've been holding ourselves back from more amply entering the realm of the other. As we slowly breathe in and out for a fourth time, we

---

8. Hasson, "Your Brain on Communication," or see Stephens et al., "Speaker-Listener Neural Coupling," 11425–30.

contemplate *Stepping Forth Wisely* into the eyes and world of the other, not with concentration but with *Fascination*.

Fascination is our doorway into *Empathy*, a tremendously useful mental paradigm. We *project less* and *absorb more*, and allow ourselves to become *Fascinated*. Instead of straining and making concerted effort we relax and ease into it, we sink into it.

A related powerful method we can use is to imagine that we're in some sense *becoming the other person*. We're still ourselves, of course, but wondering *what if we could* enlarge out beyond where we are *here* and also become closer to over *there* to where we're looking and listening? What might this feel like and permit us to realize? Thoreau once asked, "Could a greater miracle take place than for us all to look through each other's eyes for an instant?" This is what we aspire to with our practice of *Empathy*. We relax our boundaries, and with gentle intention float ourselves more over and into the realm of this other person

Before *becoming the other person*, however, even to a moderate degree, we first need to be centered within our *Self*. We don't want to become lost as we aim to more completely comprehend the other. This is where our breath awareness is yet again called upon, our foremost centering method. We first quietly breathe our awareness down into our midsection, reminding ourselves of our stable base of operation here within. Then after getting centered here inside ourselves, we can next subtly breathe our way out and into the other person, especially as we make eye contact, and while simultaneously being anchored back here in home base. This grounded centeredness quietly fortifies us for in-depth *Empathic* understanding and dialogical connectivity.

Reflecting

How does it feel when I at times background myself and foreground the other person? What's it like to practice taking off my own shoes, and then putting on and walking around in the shoes of the other? What happens as I practice gracefully "becoming the other person" while also remaining centered within myself? What are the some of the pleasures and payoffs that come from doing this?

7

The Practice of Genuineness

THE PRACTICE OF *GENUINENESS* is about being authentic and honest with others and it has two main components: (1) first, we don't pretend to be anybody we're not, and (2) secondly, we say what we honestly think and feel. So overall we're the opposite of a phony, a deceiver, a pretender. Dr. Rogers gave this overall practice his utmost respect and saw it of major importance in human relationship.[1]

Although these two elements of authenticity and honesty are intertwined in Dr. Rogers' writings, here we'll briefly break *Genuineness* into two components.

Let's start with the element of *Genuineness* that has to do with not pretending to be anybody we're not. People value and admire others who can capably serve in their "societal roles" (e.g., physician, police officer, salesperson, customer service rep, boss, professor, parent, minister, legislator, whatever) and yet at the same time be "real" persons. So part of *Genuineness* has to do with *not* hiding behind artificial professional masks, acting-out a "character," impersonally delivering a script, going by "the numbers," feigning appearances, formally keeping others at arm's distance.

The practice of *Genuineness* asks us to go past pretending at being something we're not and instead be who we actually are as a person, while at the same time functioning within our societal and organizational roles. In short, who you see is who I am, and who you get. We have our titles yet still remain human beings who put on their shoes one foot at a time like everyone else, and we humbly know this.

For example, Dr. Rogers tells about a time when he was honored to be invited to spend a year at Stanford University as a Distinguished Fellow in the Center for Advanced Study in the Behavioral Sciences. He soon found himself pretending to know more than he really did; he tried to act the

---

1. Rogers, *On Becoming a Person*, Ch. 18.

part of the "Distinguished Fellow" and project an image of expertise that exceeded his actual knowledge and confidence. He finally caught himself, dropped the false pretentions, and relaxed into being who he was. Masquerade over, time to get real, and then he felt better.[2]

The practice of *Genuineness* also has a second major component: if we're persistently thinking and feeling something across time in a relationship that matters to us (at work, in our family, with our mate, or in a dialogue group), and if we're asked what we think and feel about that something, we won't distort our truth, we won't dissemble, but will instead lean into honesty. Instead of conceal, we reveal. We find our *Genuine Voice* and let it be communicated.

This *Genuine Voicing* doesn't mean we're supposed to announce absolutely everything we're feeling and thinking all the time. Rather it's that we don't make a habit of disguising what's going on inside of us. We tell the truth of our inner experiencing especially in relationships that are *important* to us and especially if our feelings are *persisting* across time, two significant criteria here. We also attempt to accompany our *Genuineness* with *Warmth* and *Empathy*.

When it comes to expressing our *feelings*, Dr. Rogers suggested that when there's an overall alignment between (1) our real feelings, (2) our awareness of them, and (3) our outward communication of these real feelings to others, then we're being *Congruent*. That is, all three of the above levels (*feelings, awareness,* and *communication*) line-up cleanly, with no major gaps.[3]

When we're in *Congruence* we're aligned both vertically (within ourselves) and horizontally (with others). Over time people tend to respect and trust others who know and communicate what they're honestly thinking and feeling, especially when accompanied by the person-centered practices of *Warmth* and *Empathy*.

When people aren't speaking with *Genuine Voice* they're often found out. There's *nonverbal leakage* that reveals that the words they're saying out of their mouths don't match their true internal attitudes and feelings. This *leakage* might come through their lack of eye contact, their facial expression, their tone of voice, their posture, their body movement, their touch, or their other actions.

2. Rogers, *A Way of Being*, 16–19.
3. Rogers, "General Law of Interpersonal Relationships," 338–46.

In a classic study by researchers at the University of Massachusetts the *nonverbal channels of communication were found to be twenty times more important than words in the communication of Genuineness!*[4] In daily life the ratio might not always be this dramatically skewed, but the general principle holds: our nonverbal communication gets heavily weighted by others in their perception of how *Genuine* we're being.

Genuine people tend to be trusted because they're not deceiving others about what they really think and feel and need, and about who they are. They present themselves authentically and honestly. Dr. Martin Buber spoke of two main life modes, "seeming" and "being."[5] *Genuineness* is less about "seeming" and more about "being," not saying or doing one thing to our face and then saying or doing the opposite behind our back. *Genuine* people attempt to tell and be the truth, while accompanying this truth with *Warmth* and *Empathy*.

Honest presence is part of the underlying platform for dialogue. *Genuineness* and trust go together, and trust propels dialogue. Without trust we have fear, skepticism, restraint, withholding, sabotaging. The flow of dialogue is dammed up by a lack of trust. *Genuineness* when accompanied by *Warmth* and *Empathy* (an important caveat) is admired and respected and fosters trust.

In leadership research conducted all around the world involving tens of thousands of people it's been repeatedly found that the #1 characteristic people want to see in their leaders is genuine honesty.[6] More than a flashy personality, a big vocabulary, or anything else, people want to be able to trust the words and actions of those they choose to follow, and such honesty is what *Genuineness* is essentially about.

Honesty might make people slightly uncomfortable at times, but the alternative is even scarier: deception is a crazy-maker. As unsettling as *Genuine Voice* can sometimes be, it's preferable to its alternatives. We would rather hear people voice their personal truths than say things they don't really mean or believe.

In the university classroom my most *Genuine* students are also consistently among my *best* students. It's hard to be impressed by students who are letting their reticence control and contain them, but to see other students going ahead in spite of their fears and seizing *Genuine Voice* and

---

4 Tepper and Haase, "Nonverbal Facilitative Conditions," 200–04.

5. Buber, "Elements of the Inter-human," 452–54.

6. Kouzes and Posner, *Leadership Challenge*, Ch. 1.

making themselves *Vulnerable* is incredibly inspirational and valuable in the classroom. The class gets *real* when one person has the courage to be who they are, stepping-up in spite of their reservations and unveiling their *Genuineness*. Our attention is held, substance and dynamics get altered, and the entire group gets taken-up a level when authenticity prevails.

In healthy dialoguing, truth-telling and "real self-being" invigorates. We tell others our own personal truths and they tell us theirs, not as *The Ultimate Final End-All and Be-All Truth* but as *personal* truths, and subject to further change across time. Truth-telling in the short run can be awkward, yes, but in the longer run its beneficial effects are usually worth it. *Genuinely Voiced personal truth* can set others free to trust us, and reciprocate with their own truths.

Best we all be real, and say what we feel.

One of the most famous and longstanding models in the study of human communication is called the Johari Window.[7] This model highlights four areas within each of us: Public self, Private self, Blind self, and the Unknown self. *Genuineness* involves making my Private self (the part known to me but not to you) smaller across time by bringing it up into the region of my Public self, and you doing the same. *Genuineness* can also involve me giving you feedback about your Blind self (behaviors you might not be aware of) and also asking you for feedback about things that might be in my own Blind quadrant. This is the stuff of *Genuine Voicing*, and there's ample space for *Genuineness* in the province of healthy and kind-hearted dialoguing.

In addition to this, in *generative* dialoguing, where we're especially aiming to think outside the box and emerge with a broad span of images, associations, and possibilities, we need to repeatedly dare to be *Genuine* with voicing our *first* thoughts, our *first* flashes. We need to learn to get out of our own way, to stop being our own gatekeeper and seize *Genuine Voice* to forthrightly say what's passing through our mind and heart as it's happening.

Censoring ourselves endlessly instead of speaking-out sabotages creative dialogue, it falsifies the dialogue process. It's good to breathe and *Slow Down*, and *Stand Back*, and *See More*. A time comes when our dialoguing benefits from us taking the plunge into outer authenticity, so we again breathe deeply, and with *Genuine Voice* be who we are, and actually say what's on our minds and in our hearts. By so doing, we're *Stepping Forth Wisely*.

Dialoguing thrives on honesty and authenticity. When we hold back or distort what we're truly thinking and feeling, dialogue suffers. As we

7. Luft, *Of Human Interaction*.

posture and pretend to be someone we're not, or withhold who we are, we conduct a charade, and superficiality and pretense rule.

We stay stuck until some daring human beings among us bravely call upon their inner courage, daring to break the shields of distance and dissembling we've fabricated around ourselves and by which we're imprisoned. This authentic moment of truth-telling and real-self being pierces through deceptions and speaks to our consciences, our better judgment, our emotional centers, and in a shining moment at last things begin to change.

Often it's "the unspeakable" that calls for *Genuine Voicing*: transcending complacency, being real, stepping up with our personal truth and thereby invigorating the dialogue. It happened in one of my classes two days ago: multiple folks seized the chance and took a walk on the wild side of *Vulnerability* by finding and expressing *Genuine Voice*. The session became so powerful, so authentic, so real, so valuable, so human.

Human hope gleams brightly once the human spirit has again authentically spoken.

Taking Action

Find and express your *Genuine Voice* more this week than last. Say what needs to be said that no one else is saying. Somewhere, say what's on your mind and heart, and let some *Warmth* and *Empathy* be your honesty's companions. Be a personal truth-teller within a larger surround of *Caring, Accepting, Respecting,* and *Prizing* (i.e., *Warmth*) and with all the *Empathic Understanding* you can muster.

With a smile in your heart be as honest with yourself and others as you reasonably can at moments this week. Experiment with how to best tell your own *personal* truth (admittedly not *The Truth*) in a spirit of goodwill. We often wait far too long to be moved to transparency, we play it overly cautiously. At times we each need to be receptive to being overtaken by *Genuine Voicing*. May this week bring you opportunities for practice.

Dialogue scholar Dr. William Isaacs of M.I.T. urges us to ask ourselves these questions: "Can I become aware of the potential waiting to unfold through me?" "What *needs* to be expressed *now*?" "What is *my* music, and who but *I* can play it?"[8] Listen for the distant thunder, Isaacs advises, or ever so quietly listen for the deer at the edge of the woods, and then give *Genuine Voice* to what must be spoken.

8. Isaacs, *Dialogue*, Ch. 7.

Reflecting

If I'm afraid to be more transparent, what's the source of these fears? Am I willing to give these fears the voices of Squidward or Patrick or Donald Duck or Goofy or Bugs Bunny, and hear how funny they can sound as they speak to me? Can I publicly talk about my reluctances? Where might I reach within myself to draw upon the courage to practice Genuineness? Can I stand up to my self-doubt and be kindly real?

If I practice more Genuineness when wanting meaningful dialogue with others, can I envision the constructive changes that might come? How willing am I to take myself by surprise, and trust not my little "s" self but my bigger "S" Self to guide the way? Can I conceive of the possibility that I've been selling myself short? Can I dare to step into more of my undiscovered greatness?

8

The Practice of Vulnerability

I REGULARLY WATCH HEROES emerge in dialogue. In spite of their trepidations and reservations they choose to go ahead and courageously disclose themselves with *Genuine Voice*. They accept the call to adventure: they trek through the dark forest of *Vulnerability*, swim its raging rivers, cross daunting thresholds, and with *Genuine Voice* face their dragons head-on. And then they return to their dialogue community, circulating within others the life energies they've awakened, bringing boon to their partners-in-dialogue.

An exploratory dialogue can definitely be a hero's journey, very much the kind that Joseph Campbell's scholarship has so famously depicted. And as mythologist Campbell has highlighted for us, "The cave you fear to enter holds the treasure you seek."[1] Our *Genuine Voice* heroes show the rest of us the way, and first-followers are not far behind.[2] Many of the rest then come to join. Fellow stalwart journeyers lend support each to the other along the road of trials.

My recurring observation is that our dialogue heroes are not typically extraverted, outgoing, charismatic. They can often be meek and humble persons, yet when they do come to speak, others listen because their words ring real and clear. Our heroes speak from quiet ego and not to grab attention, but because there's something they feel they need to utter with *Genuine Voice* from within the forest of *Vulnerability*.[3]

They are our way-showers.

They light the way.

I will typically have several such heroes in a dialogue group. They will dare to take us places others don't. They will make their sharing real, and at times raw. They speak their personal truths and others will be silently

1. Campbell, *Hero with a Thousand Faces*, Ch. II.
2. Sivers, "First Follower: Leadership Lessons."
3. Cain, *Quiet*.

asking themselves "Is this really happening? Is this person saying what I think they're saying?" Our heroes don't stop at playing it safe; that's their beginning point, yet they don't stay stuck there. Our dialogue heroes choose to accept the call to the heroic adventure.

If you normally bypass the call to adventure in your own conversational dialoguing, I encourage you to relax into heeding the call. Be the first to take risks at times, choosing to practice *Vulnerability*, for this can, surprisingly, become among your greatest strengths. Your *Vulnerability* has been with you since birth, and now as a more maturing being you can alchemically transform your *Vulnerability* into one of your superpowers. Ironic, but true: our "weaknesses" can become our sources of awesome inner strength (e.g., honored climate activist Greta Thunberg explicitly proclaiming her OCD and mutism and Asperger's syndrome as the "superpowers" responsible for her positive global impact).[4]

As we rise to the call of adventure we gain momentum and soon discover healthy inner power. This isn't power over others but an empowerment of ourselves to transcend limitations we've too hastily bought-into in the past. We earlier capitulated to inner anxieties and fears; we weren't yet ready to warmly embrace them and courageously continue forward in spite of them.

But that was then: this is now, and this is dialogue.

Emergent leaders and first-followers create the dynamic electricity that dialoguing requires in order to surmount mere superficial chit-chat, everyone playing it socially safe and remaining fixated on appearances. Staying at that rudimentary level imperils dialoguing; someone has got to make the leap into authenticity and honesty. We need champions, we need persons gutsy enough to walk the road of trials. As Campbell has reminded us, "There is a benign power everywhere supporting the hero in their superhuman passage."[5]

But if we don't heed the call to adventure, Campbell tell us that "The refusal is a refusal to give up what one takes to be in one's own interest."[6] We then become locked in the labyrinth of our own psyche and don't get to face our dragons, at least not yet, because we timidly conclude it's not in our "best interest" to go there. This rite of passage must wait for later.

---

4. Thunberg, *No One is Too Small.*
5. Campbell and Moyers, *Power of Myth*, Ch. V.
6. Campbell and Moyers, *Power of Myth*, Ch. II.

For those who *do* heed the call to dialogical adventure, "The familiar life horizon has been outgrown; the old concepts, ideals, and emotional patterns no longer fit; the time for the passing across a threshold is at hand."[7] The dialogue hero, embodying the human spirit, makes passage to where restrictions are overcome and forgotten powers are energetically stirred to life.

Campbell further encourages us by pointing out that heroes throughout the millennia have trod the trail and faced the trials, and that "we have only to follow the thread of the hero-path." We're in historically fabulous company as we choose to reach for personal discovery and development and liberate the land with the gifts of hero-heart for all to partake of. Campbell tells us that "all the life-potentialities we never managed to bring to adult realization, those other portions of yourself, are there; for such golden seeds do not die."[8] Dialoguing gives us the chance to claim these life-potentialities, these "golden seeds," as dialogue invites us to rise to the challenge of *Vulnerability*.

Martin Buber counsels each of us is to bring ourselves fully to the dialogue, to these moments of genuine human meeting, without knowing in advance what we're going to say. In dialoguing we spontaneously and honestly disclose ourselves with *Genuine Voice*, what we think, what we feel, who and how we really are, and this is what brings our dialogical potential to life. We speak from our heart. This, of course, can make us feel *Vulnerable*.

But we don't have to feel guilty about this: we're born cautious, this is built into our DNA. Yet we don't have to choose to restrict ourselves to being biological automatons programmed by a negativity bias. We're modern humans, and *we have the capacity to choose Vulnerability* and reap its rewards. This is especially the case as we breathe our way into feeling more centered, as we continue to learn to *Slow Down*, while we take a long slow breath in and out; and as we *Stand Back*, and again slowly breathe; and also as we prepare to *See More*, as we again breathe comfortably in and out; and then an encore breath, in and out, and into *Stepping Forth Wisely*.

Let's face it: inter*personal* communication in and of itself *is* an act of intimacy (in-to-me-see), and we only ever get there through our willingness to voluntarily pivot into *Vulnerability*. To "communicate": to come into commonness of meaning, into community, into unity, into communion, into union, and all of this entails the very essence of *Vulnerability*.

7. Campbell, *Hero with a Thousand Faces*, Ch. 11.
8. Campbell, *Pathways to Bliss*, Ch. VI.

Dialoguing, fortunately for us, offers a prime opportunity to make ourselves *Vulnerable*, and at some level we already know the rewards can be worth it. Mark Nepo tells us that when salmon swim up the waterfalls each year, they do so by deliberately exposing their belly and underside to the surging oncoming current, and it's the brute force of this rushing water that propels them, in spurts, incrementally higher up the falls. Nepo keenly observes: "Their leaning into what they face bounces them further and further along their unlikely journey." Nepo refers to this as "the physics of courage," and applies it to us humans: "Time and time again, though we'd rather turn away, it is the impact of being revealed, through our willingness to be vulnerable, that enables us to experience both mystery and grace."[9]

The academic queen of *Vulnerability* is Dr. Brene Brown of the University of Houston. Dr. Brown's message is that until we choose to make ourselves *Vulnerable* to others we're holding ourselves back from such goodies as creativity, belonging, love, and joy. One of the first things we need to challenge ourselves to do, she advises, is to tell one or more persons, with our whole heart, the story of who we are, and permit ourselves to be genuinely known. When we consistently fail to do this we become numb.[10]

But as we choose to lean into *Vulnerability* we build muscles of "courage": "You can't get to courage without rumbling with vulnerability." Dr. Brown has interviewed fighter pilots, special forces troops, CIA agents, professional athletes, CEOs, activists, artists, and others, and not a single one of her respondents has ever been able to tell her a story of "courage" being demonstrated without *Vulnerability* being required.[11]

In sum, the willingness to make oneself *Vulnerable* is entailed in all great and courageous feats. And in dialogue as in life writ large courage is contagious. As we show courage by making ourselves *Vulnerable* our partners too will tend to risk their own *Vulnerability* through reciprocal courageous action. We mutually come to reveal personal details and stories about ourselves and how we see life from where we're standing now, and from where we've been in the past. We at times share privacies, imperfections, secrets, shames, revelations, all as part of our shared personal dialoguing.

This is to say *we allow our common humanness to be felt.*

We tout not so much upfront *positions* but cast light upon we *persons* who loom in the shadows behind those *positions*. We bring who we are to

9. Nepo, *Book of Awakening*, 357–58.

10. Brown, *Daring Greatly*.

11. Brown, *Dare to Lead*, Part 1.

dialogue, and at a comfortable pace let who we are be known. And in this way we find that we are more than we have thought ourselves to be.

We open-heartedly self-disclose, and so do our partners. This doesn't usually happen to any major degree in pit-stop small-talk but it happens in *person-centered* dialoguing. Piece by piece we set down our armor; we slowly come out from behind our mask; we layer-by-layer peel the onion. Pick whatever metaphor best applies to becoming more "real" and *Vulnerable*, because this is exactly what we're called upon to do as we heroically pursue the way of *person-centered* dialoguing.

As Jeremy Rifkin has said related to *Vulnerability*, "If a person locks up whole parts of their emotional make-up, they are truly unfree, imprisoning parts of their own psyche and closing off their unique being from meaningful expression and engagement with the world."[12]

But personal sharing of ourselves, our lives and feelings, is not the only way in dialogue we practice *Vulnerability*. At times we set out to have a dialogue where we want to be thinking *generatively* together, generating a wide-range of ideas, mental associations, metaphors, images, and other provocative possibilities. This is a "brainstorming" type of dialogue[13] that definitely calls out for our *Vulnerability* (see our next reading).

In everyday social talk we often we play it "safe" so as not to feel disapproval, shame, and rejection. But such preoccupations, if prolonged, can tremendously stifle *generative* (i.e., highly creative) dialoguing. Courage is required to speak without knowing exactly where we're headed, and with words and images at times running amok. This is risky business yet precisely what's needed when innovative thinking and imagining be our aim.

In *generative* dialoguing we practice *Vulnerability* by trusting dimly known yet highly resourceful parts of ourselves. We at moments get out of our own way and imagine we're letting "the muse" guide what we're saying, "as if" some grand creative nectars not of our own conscious making were pouring themselves through us. As Paul Williams and Tracey Jackson put it, "I don't know how to do this, but something inside me does."[14] We willingly make ourselves *Vulnerable* in order to trust this "something" and advance forward.

The dialogue heroes practicing *Vulnerability* and making bold forays into the unknown set the tone for others to follow, and well-serve creative

12. Rifkin, *Empathic Civilization*, 159.

13. Osborn, *Applied Imagination*.

14. Williams and Jackson, *Gratitude and Trust*, Ch. 2.

dialogue. The word "courage" comes from the Latin root *cor*, which means "heart." To be courageous is to be of strong heart in the presence of one's reluctances: to be *lion-hearted* in the face of our *fears*.

Rumi cuts to the chase and puts it boldly: "Behead yourself!" Dialogue heroes don't allow themselves to "think" incessantly; they learn to erase the excessively rational rules and habits that otherwise keep *Imagination and Improvisation* in solitary confinement. There's time enough for getting things "right" later on, if we want. But for now we know that to get to the gold we also have to let junk rocks roll-on through.

Coming to boldness and realness, that's what dialoguing is about, both when it's personal and when it's intended to be generative of a large number of novel ideas. Incessant self-consciousness and armoring are barriers, shackles of social constraint that chain us against the wall. As we begin practicing *Vulnerability* we get past our inertness and mediocrity and we awaken and our *Vulnerability* functions as our force-field going forward.

When we're committed to risking Vulnerability, the hero's journey has begun at last.

If we realize that *Vulnerability* is precisely what takes us into flourishing then we can accept whatever messiness arises, the cul-de-sacs, the stepped-on toes. We give each other permission, we mutually cut one another slack, we forgive in advance our occasionally messy *means* to our desirable *ends*.

One closing word about the hero's adventure: Michael Jordan said that he never would've set all of his basketball records if he hadn't missed 15,000 baskets along the way. To get a lot of baskets we've got to take a lot of shots. Jordan accepted the *Vulnerability* required to take the shots that ended up not going in.[15] Many shots won't succeed, but others will, and those are the ones that end up counting.

Heroes get out of their own way, and take shots that others fear to try.

So let's go for it: let's make room for *Vulnerability* in our conversations, along with the rest of our **WEG-VIBES** practices, and behold, as more of our conversations transform from an exchange of mundane monologues into rich and satisfying personal dialoguing. This choice is merely a breath and an utterance away.

---

15. Jackson and Delehanty, *Sacred Hoops*, Ch. 10.

Taking Action

What small risks can I take today that place me in positions of mild and tolerable *Vulnerability*? What other opportunities arise this week that I can use to practice becoming even more courageous? What do I hold myself back from saying or doing that might be worth a try after all? Can I go ahead and take one or more of these actions? Do I have at least three of these "going ahead" moments this week? Which of them worked out for the best, and why? What do I learn for next time? How does it feel to have some of my fears lighten their hold on me? Can I welcome any gains into my mind and being?

Reflecting

What is the toughest part of taking risks in my conversations with others? In what ways have I been playing it way too safe and as a result holding myself back? What am I learning overall about the art of taking small risks, ones not too far outside my comfort zone yet that stretch me as I go? What is the best part of taking risks and making myself Vulnerable in conversations? If I were a communication coach giving myself advice, with Warmth and Empathy, on how to deal with the challenges of conversational risk-taking, what would I say to myself?

9

The Practice of Imagination and Improvisation

IN DIALOGUE WE'RE SETTING out to be thinking *together*. I'm not having my own separate thoughts and merely expressing them in front of you, with you then independently doing the same back to me, each of us in turn displaying what's in our private brains but largely unmoved by the thinking of the other. These are technically referred to as "duologues," meaning "alternating monologues." We're each a superficially polite audience to the other, while in fact mostly waiting for our own turn to talk. This is what many people do in everyday conversations, but it's *not* collaborative dialoguing, it's not thinking *together*.

Carl Rogers once was involved in a public dialogue with a famous theologian and years later Dr. Rogers said it had been frustrating for him because he couldn't get the other participant to venture out beyond the safety of his conventional formulations: ". . . I could just see him mentally pulling out of his card file lecture number seventy-seven, and giving it."[1] Rogers saw his conversational partner delivering one monologue after another, but actual dialogue was not reached.

In this book we're largely working toward true collaborative dialoguing where 1 + 1 = 3, where two heads and hearts really *are* better than one in bringing inventive thinking and insights into existence. We transcend parading-out our old thoughts and well-rehearsed monologues and practice freshly thinking and feeling *together* now in this precious one-of-a-kind moment.

Immediately preceding another one of Dr. Rogers' public dialogues prominent social scientist Dr. Gregory Bateson was asked how he would know, by the end of it, if the dialogue between he and Dr. Rogers had been successful. Bateson immediately replied, "If either Carl or I say something

1. Rogers and Russell, *Quiet Revolutionary*, 237.

that we haven't said before, we'll know that it's a success."[2] Dr. Bateson is here alluding to this dialogical notion that 1 + 1 = 3, the whole is greater than any of its parts and even than the *sum* of its parts.

What I say triggers something within you, and then you in turn share an image or feeling or word or other association that gets generated in your mind by something I've said. Then I in turn pivot off what you've said, and we begin bouncing images and wordings and metaphors around, verbally playing together in a positive dialogical spirit, and newness emerges.

Unconventional words, sentences, thoughts, ideas, images, insights, speculations, and questions come to be born not by effortful design but evolve from our trans-active interplay. We become midwives of novel creation that we behold unfolding through us and being released into our shared world. This meeting and mixing of the minds may happen only in intermittent moments in dialoguing, yet when such precious moments do happen we've accessed the dialogical spirit. Martin Buber said "The basic movement in the life of dialogue is the turn towards the other."[3]

It's not just you, it's not just me, it's what we do *together* that takes us both past ourselves. It's not merely *communication as transmission*, as in person A to B, and person B to A, but rather persons A and B are unified in dynamic interplay and with *communication as joint creation*.[4]

What is creativity? One brief conception I like is that "Creativity is taking the old and mixing it, moving it, breaking it, or building it into newness."[5] There is a creative quality to most dialogue and therefore our math of 1 + 1 = 3. We assemble mental elements in new combinations and ways and the results exceed the "standard" (i.e., normal, predictable) total.

And *generative* dialoguing, as we're using this term in these pages, is conversation that's especially geared to maximize novel output, to spin things up a notch on the creativity dial. If I were to say to you, for example, how about a *generative* dialogue about "forgiveness," you would know I'm asking you in shorthand code for permission to think quite freely, openly, expressively, and innovatively in this topic area without judging one another's dialogical thinking.

---

2. Anderson et al., *Reach of Dialogue*, 10.

3. Matson and Montagu, *Human Dialogue*, 115.

4. Baxter and Montgomery, "Communication as Dialogue," 105–08.

5. Kirby and Goodpaster, *Thinking*, Ch. 7.

I'm asking that we minimize linear (straight-ahead) thinking and emphasize lateral (sideways) thinking.[6] I'm asking, can we be a bit off-the-wall together here, can we let our thinking run loose (and maybe even wild) in our topic area for a while and see what eventuates as we play-and-pivot off of one another?

In *generative* dialogue especially we move from a logical "top-down" mindset to a more funning around "bottom-up" mindset. We play closer to the outer edges than in a tamer dialogue, we attempt to become even more original in our seeing and saying together. Einstein famously said that problems can't be easily solved with the same style of thinking that initially created them, and therefore "We have to learn to think in a new way."[7]

Downplaying logic and evidence, in *generative* dialogue we de-focus our attention, we become softer-eyed and softer-minded. We invite our *Imagination* to become *Fascinated*, to look for connections, to envision mental associations in our mind's eye. We also let these associations and mental images flow right out here externally, to join us in this dialogical zone that we're beginning to inhabit together.

Our intention is to enter a state of creation together. We choose to operate less from left brain analysis and judgment and more from right brain aesthetic connectivity, right brain fun and flow.[8] Most all dialogue does this to a healthy degree but in *generative* dialoguing we even more abundantly call upon our practice of *Imagination and Improvisation*.

As the brilliant Ralph W. Emerson said, "The quality of imagination is to flow, not to freeze." As the **WEG-VIBES** practices are effectively enacted in highly creative dialogue we're unfreezing solid blocks of ice and transforming them into gushing waters, with *Imagination* springing forth in its free-flowing fullness. Time to slide and glide.

In this process of our *Imagination* flowing our brainwave patterns also change, with increased alpha wave production in the prefrontal cortex and activation of our mental association centers in the parietal and temporal lobes.[9] Our brains are lighting up in good spots, we're breaking free, we're liberating ourselves and one another. This is the aim of our *Improvisation* game, it's time to free us all up so our *Imagination* can freely flow.

6. De Bono, *Lateral Thinking*.

7. Einstein, *Living Philosophies*, 238.

8. Niebauer, *No Self No Problem*, Ch. 4.

9. Carson, *Your Creative Brain*, Ch. 5–7, 11.

The great Einstein knew that "Imagination is more important than knowledge." This is certainly true when it comes to acts of innovation, where *Imagination* is royalty. We respectfully honor *Imagination and Improvisation*, extending to them at least a humble hug and ideally our warm embrace.

David Bohm called dialogue the "free play" of ideas,[10] and in truly *generative* dialoguing, this is what we allow to happen. As Ray Grigg has expressed, "Playfulness is a kind of reverent disregard for imposed limits, a kind of happy defiance. It is warm spirited and positive for those with the perspective to see beyond stodgy propriety."[11]

I've taken tremendous pleasure in watching well-done comedy improvisation in L.A., San Francisco, and Chicago. Do you enjoy comedy improvisation? Creative comedy improvisation is a form of *generative* dialoguing. In comedy improvisation, as you know, a random theme is tossed up from the audience and then the improv ensemble on-the-spot and without script or rehearsal creates and acts-out a funny impromptu mini-drama, a spontaneous tragicomedy of sorts. Incredible ensemble creativity arises, and it's all playfully done in a dialogical spirit in which $1 + 1 = 3$. The whole exceeds its parts, the whole makes it happen, the whole is the show.

New elements come into being because of the playful dialogical communication between the comedic actors and their utter trust in and reliance upon human *Imagination*. One of the primary rules of comedy improvisation is that the characters are supposed to "roll" with whatever is thrown their way, to *accept* what they're given by their partners, work with it, build upon it, give it shape, and allow it to eventuate into meaningful funniness. This underlying decisive attitude of *acceptance* is what makes possible $1 + 1 = 3$.

Generative dialoguing shares common territory not only with comedy improvisation, but also with improvisational jazz and other forms of musical jamming, with contact dance improvisation, with improvisational drum circles, with freestyle rap. In these kinds of improvisational riffing and jamming events someone starts off making moves, and then other folks blend in, twisting and tweaking, spiraling out and circling back at different altitudes, rolling and floating with intoxicating unpredictability.

Each of these art forms is dialogical. Artistic creations emerge that their artists couldn't have precisely predicted from the outset. What emerges

10. Bohm, *On Dialogue*, Ch. 7.
11. Grigg, *Tao of Zen*, 320.

is not a result of cogitative pre-planning; rather it's within the process of spontaneous creation itself that the new is born.

I'm not a visual artist and I've never tried to paint anything artistic in my adult life, but my friend Steve once said, "Ron, up there above the fireplace, you should paint something." He was talking about a large vacant wall space directly above the mantle, seven feet tall by three feet wide. Accepting Steve's challenge, for five nights on the fireplace wall, six feet above the floor on a raised platform, I paint.

I paint a swirling circle, then this painted swirl gives me feedback, then I respond to what the art next seems to call out for, and then the painted wall replies, and wall and I keep working together back-and-forth like this, each continually responsive to the other, to shape an ever-morphing mutual creation that I in no way could have planned ahead of time.

My wall painting and I for five nights were dialogically dancing together, merging in artistic co-creation. For the first time in my life I received an experiential introduction to the dialogical nature of the artistic process. And, I later realized, all of the **WEG-VIBES** practices were present, and necessary!

Verbal dialoguing is an art form as well, the art of breaking free and playing together in fields of creative discourse. When we're really into playing around with our words with others, when creativity is our aim, then we're relieved of all burden to prove that what we're saying is valid, or logically follows from what another person previously said. Nor is there any felt need to justify the worth of what we're saying. We're simply abandoning ourselves to the art of verbal play as we head into exploratory inquiry.

Humans are built for play. We play in a variety of forms throughout our lives. Our sports, our entertainments, our hobbies, our recreational pursuits, our singing, our dancing, our jokes, our mutual storytelling, it's all about playing together. Across the human lifespan play is an essential element, a biological drive deep within us.[12]

And when we enter into *generative* dialoguing we're giving our need for playfulness yet another outlet for expression. We're sitting in the sandbox of mental possibilities, freely sculpting castles and roads, building exotic structures, then erasing and replacing them with still other fleeting formations. Here this moment, gone the next; now this, now that; catch me if you can, no winner, no loser, doing whatever we want in this exuberant world of mind-play.

12. Brown, *Play*, Part I.

Time-out from somber rationality, we're crossing the threshold into *generativity*. We're bouncing a beach ball or two, or three or four, and we're also playing piggyback and leapfrog with our ideas, seeing how far we can take them, and how far they'll take us. Or think of popcorn kernels warming up in the microwave, at first sporadically popping, then a whole series of popping explosions, and eventually a full bag of fresh popcorn. When the right elements are present, from a few kernels something desirable and filling pops into existence.

When dialoguing we cut one another tons of slack, we cut the chains that bind so that our minds can frolic together, *Imagination* unbound and relieved of critical judgment. In *generative* dialoguing we're having fun *Genuinely Voicing* what calls out to be uttered from our conscious, unconscious, and supra-conscious minds. That's how our popcorn pops.

What can we dream together? Will any of it make sense, anything we can later use? We don't know, no certainties here. What we do know is that playing can be fun, and research shows it's healthy for us.[13] Research also shows that those who produce the *largest number of high-quality ideas* also produce the *largest quantity of ideas overall*, many of which will be junk. It's back to Michael Jordan and missing 15,000 baskets in order to get to the ones that *will* be made.

In dialoguing we play in fields of mind knowing it'll be a hit-and-miss proposition, a price we're willing to pay to have fun surprising ourselves and spawning wacky worlds with our words. We skim surfaces, we dip into depths, we careen, we glide, we soar. How high can we fly? How will it look and feel from up there? We go for the broad bandwidth that playfulness allows. We gladden our minds and hearts, reverse the normal rules, and play anew. As Jane Wagner put it, "The human mind is kind of like a piñata: when it breaks open, there are a lot of surprises inside. Once you get the piñata perspective, you see that losing your mind can be a peak experience."[14]

We temporarily step away from rigorous critical thinking standards,[15] not because these standards are faulty, but because for now our purposes are different. In dialogue it's *okay* if we're at times *unclear, imprecise, illogical, vague, irrelevant, implausible, inconsistent,* and *incomplete,* for our intention for now is to be playing together in the fields of *generative* dialogue. So we gleefully break the normal rules in order to go far in our playful questing.

13. Brown, *Play*, Part II.
14. Wagner, AZQuotes.com.
15. See Paul, *Critical Thinking*.

My favorite photo of Albert Einstein is the one where he's riding a bicycle around in a circle outside his office and with a smile on his face. One of the most advanced intelligent minds to ever exist on the planet Earth and here he is enjoying the innocent release that *play* provides. Einstein knew how to relax, take a breath, and play at *Slowing Down*; how to breathe his way into *Standing Back,* inhaling and exhaling; and then into *Seeing More*, inhaling and exhaling; and, finally, breathing in and out and into *Riding Forth Wisely*. Even Einstein needed to change it up and breathe and play, and we do too.

I was a presenter at a "creativity in science" conference where Harvard biochemist and Nobel prizewinner Dr. George Wald was keynote speaker and he left us with these final words of advice: "As for creativity, the very heart of it is *play. Playing* IS creativity, and any scientist or artist or academic who has stopped *playing* can only hack thereafter. *Play* is infinitely important."[16]

Although play is certainly its own instant reward it also confers survival and health benefits. In many species the animals who play well together are the ones who increase their chances of survival and well-being. Play brings us to life, helps keep us alive, and awakens us to other dimensions of our being. There is a magic to playing, and as Paul Williams put it, "The magic is knowing that you've got the magic."[17] The challenge is to bring more play into our lives, and *generative* dialoguing provides us a perfect opportunity for playing in fields of *Imagination*.

How free are you personally to play with your words, your verbal imagery, your sounds, with starting your sentences without knowing where they'll end up, with making so-called "mistakes" and continuing on? As a child we reveled in letting our stream of consciousness play through, and we still can as we give ourselves permission to take flights of fancy together.

The childlike energies and brain-sets behind *generative* dialoguing include fully *Absorbing* ourselves in our topic, energetically *Connecting* elements in new ways, actively *Envisioning* images and ideas, and *Streaming* outwardly even our half-baked mental associations and insights (*ACES*).[18] These actions originate not so much from our inner Adult or Parent subpersonalities but from our inner play-loving Child, which we're choosing to at last set free. On a wooden plaque hanging in my campus office there's this

16. Wald, "Life and Mind," 14.

17. Williams, *Das Energi*, 116.

18. Carson, *Your Creative Brain*, Ch. 4.

wise inscription: "Never lose the joy of the child within you." In our *genera-tive* dialogues we're reclaiming our often hidden joy.

Yet creativity is bigger than us, larger even than our inner playful Child. Throughout history, genius inventors, composers, visual artists, literary artists, scientists, and others have written about how they eventually "forgot" themselves and got out of the way to make room for other sources or forces to come through, and in dialoguing we too *unfold* more from the *Whole*. Dr. David Bohm referred to it as making room for the *"the unlimited."*[19]

Engaging in *generative* dialoguing is a lot like being at a magic show: expectations are violated as rabbits are pulled out of seemingly empty hats, manifestations of new entities out of what seems to be nowhere. This phenomenon of the materialization of something from apparently nothing can be exhilarating.

During *generative* dialoguing the universal archetypes of the *Magician*, the *Trickster*, the *Jester*, the *Clown*, the *Fool*, and the *Muse* can be implicitly called upon and surrendered to for help in spinning our absurdities, making transformative gyrations, performing image-and-word magic by means of our *Imagination*.[20]

In *generative* dialoguing we treat logic as a limitation and scrap it for now. Time-out from normalcy and propriety, we go on a wild ride in the countryside of consciousness. We go for benign chaos, acting as if two heads (or more) are better than one and proving it yet again. We strive for unexplored and freewheeling directions off the beaten path. We get to "Aha!" moments, gamma signals bursting in our brains.

The distinguished physicist Niels Bohr once tried to cajole his colleague, the renowned Einstein, to reach for even more creative thinking in a given situation by taunting, "You are not thinking. You are merely being logical." In *generative* dialoguing we throw away logic and proof for the moment and see what we come up with unhindered by straight-laced rules. Our motto essentially becomes "Everything we think we know is partial or wrong" and this liberates us to start over from the beginning.

We're members of Team Human and therefore both highly communicative and imaginative. We can rise above, reach below, and reach past our logical and critical minds and together midwife innovative insights into this world, and this may be what saves us.

19. Bohm, *On Dialogue*, 92–94.
20. See Gilbert, *Big Magic*.

We have done this, can do this, and will continue to do this.

Carl Rogers saw our creative urge as springing from our inborn directional tendency to express and extend ourselves, to strive for personal development, to activate our capacities to their fullest, to actualize who and what we can become.[21] Dialoguing asks us to make this actualizing choice: to play, to dream aloud, to use our *Imagination and Improvisation* to create together with other human beings. Through dialoguing we not only further actualize ourselves but one another and our relationship, as we again demonstrate that, yes: 1 + 1 can = 3.

In multiple senses simultaneously, something more is born between us.

Taking Action

We let our mind run freer today even when in casual conversations with grocery clerks, janitors, strangers, service reps, mail persons, wait persons, secretaries, folks at the copy machine. We're not aiming for sustained *generative* dialogue in these mini-interactions, we're using them as runways from which we can practice brief flights of *Imagination and Improvisation*. Our dialoguing can be momentary. We improvise on the spot, coming up with more zany off-the-wall funniness than usual and noticing how much lightness and connection this brings.

We cease being so literal and serious and "let our hair down," joking and playfully teasing with kindness and rascality. The *Warmth* we exude communicates that we're of goodwill and intend well. We get out of our own way, we don't cogitate so much, we have a smile on our face and in our voice and we discover what can happen as our tension somewhat dissolves. We invite short and fun dialogical mini-interludes over the span of our days and weeks. We let this become our new art form: brief episodes of *generative* conversation even if for a few seconds at a time, leaning into dialogical creativity.

And in more in-depth conversations that come our way we at times ask the other person whether we can both can be a little more playful and *generative* than usual. We give one another a green light, a go-ahead signal, so that we can explore more openly without premature closure and negative judgment, simply for the fun of it and for what it might yield (and that we can later discuss more rationally if we so choose).

21. Rogers, *On Becoming a Person*, Ch. 19.

In dialoguing we ask for and give the other expanded space in which to inquire and roam. Our dialogue will end up all the better because we choose to give and receive a healthy dose of added spaciousness.

Reflecting

I begin to understand that dialogue can come in many sizes and durations. I can have spurts of dialogical interactivity throughout my days in informal moments, not only in more formally structured dialogue situations. I see that I can be dialogical with someone in fifteen seconds of clock time as we briefly volley together, not to score points but to keep the ball aloft.

We play around together, we create fun thoughts, words, images, and ideas, and we can do this within seconds. This brings pleasure, vitality, value, relief, and hope. And now and again it also brings insights, answers, and more questions. Advocacy closes, and dialogue opens. I open my mind and heart and arms to embrace the dialogical, to 1 + 1 = 3.

10

The Practice of Being Now and Here

THESE DAYS THERE'S TONS of emphasis on the importance of being able to clearly focus our attention on what's happening in the *present moment* where we are, and without heavy corrective judgment. This is the essence of "mindful presence." Whether in sports, musical performance, art, hobbies, public speaking, lovemaking, cooking, gardening, or whatever, being able to immerse oneself nonjudgmentally in the present moment of action is useful and gratifying. It's tied into the state known as "flow" where we're "in the zone" and operating smoothly, efficiently, and effectively, and we feel alive and great.[1]

Conversational dialoguing also benefits from mindful present-centeredness. If our minds are rewinding our past history or fast-forwarding into the future we'll miss the rhythm and beat of this here-and-now conversation and fall out of step. Having our bodies in attendance but our minds elsewhere blocks dialoguing. If we're half present but half not we'll falter and stumble. To get completely synchronized with our dialogue partners and upgrade mere small talk to the level of authentic *shared inquiry*, we need to practice *Being Now* and *Here*.

Yet it remains a fact of life that even when wanting to pursue dialogue our attention will often tend to drift. We'll come and go with our daydreams, sensations, thoughts, worries, irritations, feelings, and fantasies, swept away to other times and places. This is not our personal failure, but rather the habitual tendency of the Western mind; research shows that most folks in conversation are about 50 percent present, and 50 percent elsewhere.

So we *practice returning*. Whenever we finally notice we've drifted off, it's our *practice* is to come back to an awareness of our breathing in, and out, right here in this nanosecond. We do this to help us recurrently return

1. Brown et al., *Handbook of Mindfulness*, Ch. 1.

to entering the dimensionality of this present moment, to *Being Now* and *Here*. Ancient Eastern wisdom from more than a thousand years ago put it this way: "To become conscious of inattention is the mechanism by which to do away with inattention. Laziness of which a person is conscious, and laziness of which they are unconscious, are a thousand miles apart."[2]

As we become aware of our distracted focus and gently return our body-mind presence to *Being Now and Here* we are in this microsecond doing reps to fortify our re-focusing muscles. We're strengthening our mental biceps for focused awareness each and every time we return. Our flights of fancy provide us opportunity for developing mindful presence as we *learn to return* to *Being Now* and *Here*.

I used to have a friend from Japan whose father had held a ninth degree black belt in a martial art. I asked her what was the most important martial arts lesson she'd ever learned from her father. She answered, "Return to Stance." She explained that it's not so much whether we lose our centered, poised, balanced stance in the martial arts, but how efficiently we're able to "Return to Stance." Even the master is not perfect and can at times lose their presence, but the master is skilled at recognizing this and then quickly coming back to balanced stance and *present-centeredness*.

Healthy energizing power in dialoguing springs from *Being Now, Here*. When we find we've wandered off in our head *we soon become aware that we're aware of this*, and we then return to *feeling* (and not merely thinking about) our body breathing in and out, and return to sensing that *here we are now*, doing precisely this. We "Return to Inner Stance," inner poise, this unrepeatable existing moment. Our perception becomes cleaner; we hear more, notice more, sense more.

Being Now and *Here* can provide sensations of lightness and vibration, dynamic stillness, clarity and vivacity, a settling down into our listening. Present-centeredness can seem to slow the passage of time, each moment becoming more bountiful. Our loving acceptance of the other person(s) often heightens, an awareness of profound connection occurs, our absorption in our dialogue intensifies, and a sense of the sacred arises (e.g., humility, awe, reverence).

Dialoguing can at its highest moments become a *peak communication experience*.[3] Such moments are fleeting and rare and we cannot hope to

2. Wilhelm and Jung, *Golden Flower*, 47.
3. Gordon, *Tuning-In*, 309–12.

long dwell in such magical dialogical moments, yet we can savor them as they come to greet us in the *Here Now.*

To return to present-centeredness during dialogue repeatedly is our *practice,* and we continually renew our practice of this *practice.* We don't want to only be re-cycling through re-runs of old *thoughts* from days gone by, we want to be buzzing in the current of present-centered *thinking.* And we want to *feel* what's passing through us right at this second, not be trapped by "felts" from yesteryear. We want to step into the present-centered energetic field at the exact moment of dialoguing, stepping into the pure experience of *Now* and *Hear.*

Again, it's normal to repeatedly stray from present-centeredness: it's our *return* that's our training in refocusing, and our *return* that brings added fullness of presence to our dialoguing. Sleepwalking automatons don't dialogue; dialoguing is left to fully alive *Here and Now* beings.

Breath awareness is one of our very best doors for returning to *Being Now* and *Being Here.* The great Dr. William James, one of the founding fathers of American psychology, put it succinctly over a hundred years ago: "The instant field of the present is at all times what I call the 'pure' experience." James went on to in essence argue that, "I breathe, therefore I am." Not "I think therefore I am" or "I logically argue, therefore I am" but rather my *breathing* is the most elemental true fact of all, and straight at the center of the pure "I am" experience.[4]

The scientific research on breath awareness practice is by now extensive and demonstrates significant positive effects, especially in the areas of mind-wandering, focus training, empathy enhancement, stress reduction, boosting the immune system, heart health, pain reduction, fear management, depression and trauma treatment, and the list goes on.[5]

Eastern philosophy has for over three thousand years positioned breath awareness prominently as the supreme tool for accessing the majesty of present-centeredness.[6] Some religious scholars have gone further, noting that the Buddha taught that with breath awareness practice a person can enter into a state of enlightenment. Even though our aims here are more moderate, it's reassuring and empowering to know of the tremendous tradition and force behind this simple practice of breath awareness.[7]

4. James, *Essays and Lectures*, 136–37.

5. Goleman and Davidson, *Altered Traits*; Brown et al., *Handbook of Mindfulness.*

6. Watts, *Way of Zen*, 198.

7. Nhat Hanh, *Breathe, You Are Alive*, Ch. 1.

From both Western scientific research and ancient Eastern wisdom teachings, then, breath awareness is a practice worth cultivating within the larger practice and state of *Being Now, and Being Here*. Yet the use of breath awareness relates not only to *Being Now and Here* alone but to all of our other **WEG-VIBES** practices as well. Our breath awareness can assist us in *Suspending*, support us in putting into practice *Genuineness* and *Vulnerability*, enable us the patience grant others *Equality of Participation*, and so on down the line.

This is why we revisit breath awareness repeatedly in this book: it's an across-the-board asset, our omnipresent friend and ally, including for bringing us into the electrically-charged field of the *Now and Here*. I especially encourage you to let your exhalations be slow and long. Deeply inhale a breath through your nostrils all the way down into your belly, then, try this: purse your lips as if you're drinking through a straw, and now slowly release your outbreath through your pursed lips. Try this pursed lips technique now, three to five times, eyes closed.

Enjoy the afterglow in this immediate moment.

Prominent neurological researcher Dr. Stephen Porges tells us it's our slow exhalations in particular that down-regulate our sympathetic nervous system and allow us to become calmer, relaxed, and present-centered.[8] Relaxing our body relaxes our mind, takes pressure off our defense circuits, and measurably supports our health, restoration, and growth.[9]

A worthwhile resource in steeping ourselves in the practice of present-centeredness is the website of the UCLA Mindful Awareness Research Center with beneficial no-cost guided focusing activities as well as a weekly podcast.[10] I also recommend the book written by two of the Center's directors.[11] Other useful mindfulness resources are listed in the Bibliography.[12]

If you turn to none of this, no problem, but do *return to feeling your breathing*. This is what matters. Your conscious breathing regenerates you, and brings you back to *Now*. Drop down beneath your head and mind and thoughts and into the heart of your breathing body. Your breathing body becomes your entryway. So *Slow Down* inside yourself, pause, and breathe

---

8. Porges, *Polyvagal Theory*, 185–94.

9. Van der Kolk, *Body Keeps the Score*, Parts I and II.

10. MARC at uclahealth.org.

11. Smalley and Winston, *Fully Present*.

12. See Ferguson, *Natural Wakefulness*; Jon Kabat-Zinn, *Coming to Our Senses*; Kornfield, *The Wise Heart*; Brach, *True Refuge*; Tart, *Living the Mindful Life*; Goleman, *Focus*.

in and out; and *Stand Back* within as you again enjoy inhaling, and exhaling; and next, imagine you can *See More* as you take another breath in, and out; and finally, *Step Forth Wisely* by breathing your way into your body in precisely this moment and place *Now & Here*.

Silences in dialogical conversations are especially prime sites for returning to our breath awareness. Silence offers an unspoken invitation to return to feeling our bodily presence in our chair, our feet on the floor, our chest rising and falling, and air coming into our nostrils and out our mouth. This can all be done quite subtly, with eyes open, and without calling undue attention to itself.

But silence is more than a chance to practice breath awareness. Silence has its own qualities, textures, meanings, levels, dimensions, clarities, and possibilities.[13] Ancient Chinese sage Chuang Tzu put it well for our purpose of dialogue: "And if water thus derives lucidity from stillness, how much more the faculties of the mind?"[14] Silence in dialogue can be the stilling of the waters from which everyone's mind derives benefit.

In most conversations people minimize silences because they're thought of as awkward and uncomfortable. We at times avoid silences like the plague, or rupture silences prematurely due to the anxiety they trigger. There's an intimacy entailed in being silent together, and often people don't want to allow themselves or their partners to feel this implied intimacy. Silences are often abruptly broken.

Yet when we do allow ourselves to luxuriously recline into shared silences they can be among the most connective parts of dialogical conversation. If all present to our dialogue are patient and courageous, *Genuine Voice* and heart-full energies can emerge from unrushed natural silences.

Silences in dialogue can bring us a mood of unspoken community.

Silences can become portals into mysterious dimensions of *Being Now* and *Here*.

Silences can become paradoxical voids out of which deep communication flows.

In dialogical conversation we're encouraged not to run from silences out of reflex habit but to hang-in there for a while, to scoot down into whatever experiences the silence is bringing. We can learn to welcome unfamiliarity and weirdness head-on as we experiment with settling back and into our more protean possibilities.

13. Sardello, *Silence*.
14. Watson, *Chuang Tzu Basic Writings*, Section 19.

As we learn to first endure, and then to enjoy, entering into the silences in our dialogical conversations, we find ourselves in fertile terrain. Silences can be moments for laying the groundwork for profoundly meaningful sharing. Dr. Bohm goes so far as to advise us that silences are *essential* for the occurrence of maximum *coherence*. He speaks of cultivating "empty spaces": "So we have here a kind of empty space where anything may come in, and after we finish, we just empty it. We are not trying to accumulate anything."[15] We sometimes ride with our silences, we feel our way into them, and we communicate from within them, unrushed and when the moment is right. They are not an interruption to an agenda, for dialogue is ultimately agenda-less.

Yet even when there aren't many external silences we can still let there be a half-minute of internal silence within ourselves now and again. We can embody our own personal silences, smoothly surfing our breathing, occupying our body, resting in open heartfelt awareness. In such moments inner restoration is underway, and we gladly learn to become receptive to it.

We silently bring ourselves back into the vivacity of this living moment, the eternal present. Mental fantasies and *there-and-then* talk are okay for a while, but the real *energia* resides in the *Here* and *Now*. This is where vibrancy and fire are found, so we *practice returning*, and our outer and inner silences provide renewed opportunity.[16] Then from within this *Now* and *Here* we can emerge, more purely speaking from our heart-mind what we're authentically sensing, feeling, and wondering, allowing it to freely flow.

Taking Action

So we can use naturally occurring silences to scoot down into *Being Now and Here*. In our noisy world we forget about silence; we even become intimidated by it, often scared of it. Befriending silence can become our way of returning to *Being Now and Here*. We can also realize that the *eternal moment* does not stretch out before us in lineal time, it is not a horizontal phenomenon, rather it is *vertical*: *Here* is eternity now, and we listen to *Hear* now.

We use our breath awareness as a tool for bringing our mind back to where we are physically *Now and Here*. We do this several times in our day. We make it an ongoing part of our life, allowing mind and body to

15. Bohm, *On Creativity*, Ch. 4.

16 Abram, *Spell of the Sensuous*, Ch. 2; also see Abram's *Becoming Animal*, 159–81.

again unify. There's no sophisticated technique to be mastered, all we do is recall we're breathing and then *feel* our body breathing, air rushing into our nostrils, and out our mouth.

Also at times during our dialoguing, or in our day, we might ask ourselves silently or softly, "*What time is it?*" and then give ourselves the answer "*Now.*" Then we ask ourselves, "*Where am I?*" and answer the question "*Here.*" We go beyond perfunctory answers and actually *feel* and accept the truth of what we're saying, for truer words were never spoken. We ask, and then be silent for 15 to 30 seconds and soak-in our answers. This can help bring us back to where we need to *Be.*

Another good question we can use to come back to where our body is located in space and time is this one by mindfulness teacher Loch Kelly: "*What's here now when there's no problem to solve?*" Putting this question to ourselves, framed this way, and backing into a *felt answer*, can often settle us down into the comfortability of the present moment and what Kelly calls "awake awareness."[17]

Eckhart Tolle uses another quick method, inviting us to close our eyes and ask ourselves this question: "*How can I know right now that my right arm is really here?*" *Feel* your way into your answer. Next, after 15 to 30 seconds or so, and if you want, "*How can I know that my left arm is here?*" Then, if we choose, to the feet, legs, torso, and head. These questions prompt us to do a brief internal body scan and begin to make contact with our embodied world of sensation, which brings us to more life *Here* in *Now.* In fact, awareness of our right arm alone can often be enough to efficiently achieve this.[18]

Reflecting

I know that as I hang out in my head with my worries, anxieties, daydreams, fantasies, remembrances, I take myself out of the Now and Here. Caught up in the erratic reruns and dramas in my own head it's hard to be available for thinking together with others. When I find that I've strayed off again, entangled in a swamp of inner details and debris, I become aware of this and bring myself back by consciously breathing, bodily feeling my way into Being Now and Here.

17. Kelly, *Effortless Mindfulness*, Ch. 6.
18. Tolle, *Power of Now*, Ch. 6.

This becomes an enjoyable game of sorts, finding myself not being present and then bringing myself back to Here and Now yet again. A focusing workout and a game, both at the same time. I easily discover that my presence in the immediate moment enhances my perception and possibilities, compared to when I'm distracted and split. I continue to make the inevitable return, and in so doing automatically unify my capacities. Awareness makes it so.

11

The Practice of Equality
of Participation

THIS PRACTICE CAN BE among the most difficult of the *WEG-VIBES* practices to sustain. It is so tempting for we humans to want to hear ourselves speaking, and receive the hormonal hit of dopamine in our brain that we get from telling our own stories. It's understandable with this built-in physiological reward system that we will at times want to hog the floor. But stage-hogging impedes dialogue, and needs to be continually be brought back into awareness and actively managed by one and all, for the good of the whole.

Think of an ordinary Christmas tree bulb. Know that when the light from this rather innocuous bulb is collected together into a gathered beam of *coherent* light this energy beam becomes powerful enough to penetrate a thin sheet of steel. *Coherence* entails unification, a bringing together of all the rays of light. A major way that a two-person dialogue or a dialogue group achieves *coherence* is by striving to honor and implement the norm of *Equality of Participation*. This is a step toward attaining our laser-like strength.

In any conversation the question implicitly arises, "Who's going to get the attention here, how are we going to allocate attention?" We don't pose this question outwardly, but by our conversational behavior we answer it. We answer it by how *talk-time* gets distributed. Quite often, certain conversationalists end-up "rich," they get tons of *talk-time* attention from the others present, and some people end up "poor," they get only scant conversational attention and are rendered invisible.[1]

I'm recalling a student I'll call Brandon. I like Brandon a lot, and at the same time I'm aware there are things Brandon could be working on if he's ever going to further develop as a dialogical communicator. For instance,

1. Derber, *Pursuit of Attention*, Part I.

73

Brandon would shoot his hand and arm straight up into the air and keep it held high the entire time someone else would be holding the floor and speaking to our class. During several sessions I let Brandon know he could put his hand down and be assured he'd get his turn next, that I'd remember he wanted to talk, but he found it hard to want to put his hand down. Brandon had an ego that clamored for attention: "Look at *Me*, listen to *Me*, *I'm* here, somebody to be reckoned with, get to *Me*, *I* have points to make, come on, feel *My* impact, get to it, let's here from *Me* again."

Yet twenty other people were present too, but Brandon wasn't nearly as concerned with seeing and hearing and feeling most of *them*. They were not his real focus: Brandon was more preoccupied with making his own impression on others, repeatedly. This style can make for a lively "Brandon Show" session but it's not conducive to dialogue. For real dialogue to occur, we need to abandon repetitive center-stage ego-glorification performances: no superstars here, no grandstanding sought.

I'm also thinking of a middle-aged returning student, Janelle, who could produce multiple compelling five-minute soliloquies in a single session that would captivate the class's attention and impress them with her verbal talents. The problem was that Janelle's colorful self-absorptions tended to stifle others who didn't feel as articulate or charismatic, and who would then over-rely on her as our starring lead character. Plus, it crowded-out others from getting *talk-time* too, it left them in the shadows.

When our aim is dialoguing, repeated and extended monologues don't cut it. Instead, everyone needs to be respectfully and fairly included as an *equal* member of the dialogue, each with a vital and *equal* part to play.

If authentic dialoguing is to occur, charismatic extraverted folks need to practice stepping down from the pedestal, learn to stop holding the spotlight mostly on themselves, and learn to give the gift of attention to others. This is the democracy of dialogue, where egos work to quiet themselves and allow graciousness to arise. The monopolizing few gracefully bow out of center-stage and practice other roles and skills they're less familiar with and need to acquire, like giving attention to another person and deeply listening. Everyone grows, and we all gain.

In their efforts at dominating, one of the main tools that *conversational narcissists* use is the *shift-response*, where you tell me something about your morning or day or life and I reply *not* by asking you to "tell me more" about your experiencing, but by rushing in to tell you *my own comparable story*: "Yeah, that happened to me before too, only it was even worse . . ." I match your story, and try to top it when I can. That's quite often the intention of the person *shift-responding*, not merely to say in a few words that they "get it" and can relate, but to launch into the details of their own semi-related story and divert attention from the initial speaker.[2]

In the guise of empathy the *shift-response* show is again underway. *Genuine Empathy* can be conveyed by a single concise verbal sentence along with sincere nonverbal *Empathic* communication, including supportive eye contact and vocal tone, resonant facial expressions, and heartfelt body language. We don't need to steal attention from another person with our own matching story to show that we can relate; there will be a more opportune time for our own tale.

Conversational narcissism runs rampant in our individualistic culture, it's epidemic. Few articulate conversationalists are willing to also hear-out someone else, to allow the other person to also be the center of attention for a while. Yet in dialogue this is precisely what needs to happen. We need to practice *support-responding* rather than *shift-responding*, to be able to say, "Say more about that if you can" "What else happened?" "How did this make you feel?" "What did you learn from that situation?" "What insights does it lead you to?" "Talk about how that relates to what we spoke about earlier" "What questions did this raise for you?" "Tell me more, yeah?"

With *support-responses* we avoid getting in a tug-of-war for attention. We keep our *focus* on the other person until they finish their expressing, and even then maybe we invite them to "Tell us more." We don't *shift-respond*, implicitly saying "Hey, we've spent 15 seconds on you already, now you look over here and listen to ME again!" We downplay tendencies to want to *shift-respond* and instead morph our words into forming *support-responses* that sustain attention on the other person.

And we hope at the right times our conversational partners will reciprocate. If they're honestly practicing dialoguing, they'll strive to balance talk-time *equally* overall.

Countless times I've seen that when a few powerful figures dominate a group, this power imbalance eventually results in resistance. Nobody knows everything, but some folks act like they do, and this usually doesn't work out so well for them or us in the longer haul. A dominating personality who delivers compelling monologues at first entertains, but past a point falls flat, and the aftertaste hovers unpleasantly sour. Power inequalities

---

2. Derber, *Pursuit of Attention*, Ch. 1–2.

THE WAY OF DIALOGUE

prevent the fair and full participation of other voices, and people come to realize and resent this.

Research shows that "expressive talkers," those talented at "the gift of gab," have *less influence* on other people in the long run than communicators who are especially skilled at *listening*. Good *listeners* are appreciated for being attentive to other peoples' needs, and their positive *influence* lingers. So while both skills matter, speaking and listening, listening is the more neglected skill in most cases, and the one making the most lasting mark. Good listening lingers in the mind.

Time to round it out: folks who deliver too many unidirectional monologues need to drop-back and practice listening, and those folks who are routinely reticent in conversation need to practice finding their *Genuine Voice* and speaking up. Each participant in a genuine dialogue is challenged to actively exercise their personal *Genuine Voice* in proper proportion to the Whole. Dialoguing is given birth, nourished, and reaches fruition when everyone present receives ample opportunity to take responsibility for bringing dialogue into being.

Sometimes active talkers will let there be five or so seconds of silence after they've finished talking, and then if no one else quickly rushes in to say anything they or another highly active talker will again take control of the group. This can be made to seem like, "Well, you had your chance, and if you're not going to go for it, then that's your problem, so here I go again . . ."

The assumption that a five or ten second pause is long enough and then needs to be filled is *not* the operative assumption in dialogue. We learn to let silences exist, to be there, and we allow words and feelings and moods and reflections to sink-in during these rich junctures. We can, with practice, come to welcome, enjoy, and luxuriate in our shared silences.

Often our silences will enable a transition into contributions from quieter persons who haven't been talking so much because they felt no doors remained open long enough through which they could make their way. In dialogue a silence might last for thirty seconds, a minute, or more, and if we outgoing folks don't hastily crash in to fill it, meaningful material can arise from such silences, and at times fresh voices. We learn to be patient and wait, and see what will happen. We learn to make space, and treasure our silences together.

Silences also provide the perfect opportunity to remember we're breathing, to wake up to and *feel* our body's breathing. We do so as we *Slow Down,*

Stand Back, See More, and then *Step Forth Wisely* from there. This can fortify us to quiet down, or to get ready to speak up, as the group needs.

Another faulty assumption is that dialogue has to consist of lengthy verbal exchanges: this is not true. For example, examining a transcript of a dialogue between David Bohm and his dialogue partner J. Krishnamurti on the weighty topic of "Mind in the Universe" we find that over 90 percent of their contributions were only one, two, or three short sentences in length, and one-sentence contributions were the most frequent of all. And of the less than 10 percent of the contributions that were longer than three sentences, their average length was only five sentences, not so long after all.[3]

The quiet ego learns to speak concisely, and keep the dialogue dynamically moving along. Everyone practices *Equality of Participation* and people's needs and rights to be heard get equally met. Dialogue is *not* about the survival of the loudest, the longest-winded, and the quickest to speak. Dialogue is *not* about the magnification of parts but about the Whole becoming a Whole.

When each and all of the parties to the dialogue are permitted to fully function then dialogue takes root in fertile soil. Ego resists this of course and can get loud and cranky: "How can *I* give equal time to *you* when what *I've* got to say is so much more important and valid?" But we can actually learn to take satisfaction in quieting down our ego and allowing others to step in. It takes practice, but can be done.

Everyone in dialogue would do well to work at becoming "lean of speech" during any single turn. Many people, whether extroverted or introverted, hold the floor for too long once they have it. We can each benefit from streamlining our delivery. The fact is, we'll be even more impactful as we trim excess verbiage, and more well-regarded within our dialogue. We need to learn fair turn-taking, and to be concise during any single turn. These are important guidelines when pursuing the way of dialoguing.

Coherence develops as a team draws upon all of our resources, not only a select fraction from among them: "all for one, and one for all." And as Thich Nhat Hanh has noted, "To see one in all and all in one is to break through the great barrier which narrows one's perception of reality."[4] But the one should not crowd out the all, or then we see only that one, and not at all the all. Equality is the answer, greater balance the way.

3. Krishnamurti and Bohm, *Ending of Time*, 234–50.

4. Hanh, *Art of Communicating*, Ch. 4.

And ultimately the place, the location, that we aim for as we speak in our dialogue circle is the physical and psychological center of our circle, not the outer rim where we're all sitting. We eventually begin to speak less to one individual at a time and increasingly to the center of our circle where we all overlap and join. We speak from within the Whole to the Whole. We graduate beyond separate personalities; we aim to hear meanings flowing through from a larger Whole.

I often tell my groups that our exact dialogue group will never exist again on the planet Earth, that we, this precise convergence of persons and personalities, is an unrepeatable event. May we fully sense, utilize, and enjoy the unique convergences of which we are a part, while we're able to.

And can we let the systems theory axiom that "the Whole is *greater* than the sum of its parts" not only be something we intellectually accept but a truth we're witnessing and living? This tantalizing possibility speaks to us, teases us, lures us. Are we willing, up close and personal, to sense more of our distinctive Wholeness? Can we let our mutual "turning toward" each other bring us into moments of realizing our larger "Between-ness"?

And if by chance we're letting the Whole become *less* than the sum of its parts, then we've clearly got work to do in becoming more Whole. Drawing others forth in our dialogue becomes our worthwhile project. We want to be balanced in our dialoguing, to cultivate the strength of each of our parts and put them together rightly, so we can ascend to the next level in upward spiral. We return to equality, to fair proportion, to assist us in reaching our dialogical potential for contact and connection.

Taking Action

It's time to watch how we're handling the distribution of *talk-time* in our communication relationships. Look and see: if we're in a pair, are we consistently taking more than about 50 percent of the total available *talk-time*? If we are, let's take our foot off the accelerator. We lapse back, *project* less, *absorb* more. One of the biggest lessons a majority of communicators still need to learn is to grandstand less, and *listen* to others more wholly.

If we're in a dialogue group we might consider making the following rule together: no one can speak three times until everyone else present has spoken at least once (the "buffet table" guideline, no thirds until others get their first turn). And we might want to consider asking everyone to approximately sustain that 3:1 ratio (or another reasonable ratio) as we all continue on. We know that conversational narcissism destroys dialogue, and needs to be minimized for the sake of the Whole.

In dialogue, each person needs to begin to monitor how they, and others, are occupying and yielding *talk-time*. We activate our self-awareness within this area. If we find that our talk-time ratio with others is out of whack, we balance it out for the sake of our self, others, and the dialogue. Again, some folks need to *project* less and *absorb* more; others need to *absorb* less and *project* more. Where are we? We self-observe, and also ask others for feedback, and find out.

If we're the quiet one, the introvert, the participant who says little, our task is not to say even less but to *find our voice* by speaking it. We're challenged to *not* remain a sponge for others, to *not* only be a good receptive listener, but to also have insights to offer through our own distinct voicing and wordings. We need and deserve to be heard our fair share; what we say could matter. There are things that only we can say in our way, and withholding them could hamper the entire dialogue process. Just as we don't want to dominate, we don't want to disappear.

If we're on the reserved side, then our heroic journey is *to find, and project, our voice*. We start to make our voice heard, our presence felt. We give people a better feel of us, and the more they know of us the more they'll trust and feel connected with us. We silent folks can be scary to people because they don't know "what's going on" inside us. So we relieve others of their trepidations, uncertainties, and false interpretations. Putting our self "out there" promotes the dialogue, so we do our part by actively taking part in the dialogue. We transcend passivity, and humanely assert our presence.

Whichever direction in which we're lopsided (if in fact we are), it's time to round-it-out for the sake of dialogue. Awareness is key: we breathe in and out as we *Slow Down,* as we *Stand Back,* as we *See More,* and as we then *Step Forth Wisely*. These four simple breath cycles, in and out, can help us move into balance.

In a group dialogue one of the responsibilities of the facilitator is to serve as an orchestra conductor, to summon the instruments "over there" to make their presence more noticeably heard and experienced, and to appeal to the instruments "up here in front" to tone it down for the good of the music of the Whole.

But the ultimate is for each of us to learn to do this for ourselves, since we won't always have a conductor in the pit.

Reflecting

I begin to notice, and inquire into, how much I talk and how much I listen when I'm with others, especially when I want to be heading in a dialogical direction. Am I crowding others out, cutting them off, or sincerely inviting them in and giving them room? Am I dominating? Am I shift-responding to show my Empathy, but then letting my story get away from me?

Or am I being too soft-spoken, depriving the others, not sharing enough of myself, what I think, what I've learned, what I feel?

Am I willing to ask the other(s) their views of me on all this? Am I amenable to tweaking my behaviors here, to get it "just right" in any given instance? Through the light of my awareness, can I strive for healthy balance of inflow and outflow?

12

The Practice of Suspending

HERE'S AN EXERCISE WILL help illustrate what it means to be *Suspending*. Pick up a pen, or pencil, or your ring, or any other small object. Go ahead and get your object, I'll wait.

Now, grip this object tightly, a stranglehold clench, shut your hand around it and squeeze. Use muscle, really squeeze it hard, and go for twenty or so seconds here. And as you squeeze notice how this tightness feels in your hand and arm, in your jaw and face, in other body parts, and how this affects your mind, and your breathing. Observe how much it binds and constricts you physically, mentally, and emotionally to clench this object so hard, to be so fused with it.

Next, ease up slightly, softening your grip, ever so gently unfolding your fingers in slow motion, enjoying the incremental transition, backing off of the tension, gradually lightening up. Take your time. Relish this de-fusion process every millimeter of the way. Let your body breathe. Savor the process of letting go, and ever so slowly extending your fingers, but with the object still in your palm.

You've just *Suspended* your grip on the object. You've let most of the tension be released. You still have the object in your hand, but you're not bound-up and contracted by your inflexible relation with it. Now playfully let your object roll around in your hand a bit, and even toss it up a half-inch or so into the air above your palm. Notice your relationship with this object now. Notice how you can experience this object more completely when you're not clinging to it with all of your force. You're now in a more relaxed relation with your object, and can come to know it even better. Breathe another sigh of relief. (And if you haven't done the above object exercise yet, please do so now, before you continue reading.)

Imagine if this pen or other object was the equivalent of a belief, an opinion, an assumption, a conclusion, an argumentative stance, a position.

To *Suspend* it means to hold it less tightly, with less desperation and frantic attachment. *Suspending* is not abandoning the opinion or point of view, but simply relaxing our grip on it for the time being. We can always return to our tight grip later on if we so choose, but for now, for the purposes of dialoguing, we choose to *Suspend* clenched grip and hold more lightly.

As Hugh Prather once observed, "It is impossible to make a general statement that covers every exception, and yet conversation so often consists of each person pointing out the obvious exceptions to the other person's statements."[1] Those who yearn for more than "You're wrong, I'm right" conversations are fine candidates for person-centered dialogue, and *Suspending* is a vital part of the process. We make more "space" around our beliefs and judgments, we center ourselves and create more breathing room.

In dialoguing we often want to go beyond staying glued to what we already "know," and instead practice *Suspending*.[2] Especially when setting out to have a highly creative dialogue, we want to invite wilder mind, we want to tinker with possibilities, to twiddle around, to dabble, to toy with images and words and ideas, to mess around with thoughts and language and imagery and associations and see what, if anything, all this might yield.

In order to do this, for the time being we practice letting go of our tight grip and *Suspending* our intact beliefs and opinions and typical ways of seeing and thinking and feeling. We are instead taking a walk on the wild side of creative minding. As Thomas Edison advised us long ago: "To have a great idea, have a lot of them." It's our *Suspending* that allows us not to get wedged into any solitary idea or mental place for too long, and that opens us out into wider-angle seeing and kaleidoscopic thinking.[3]

With *Suspending* we extend ourselves beyond our normal limiting assumptions and stopping points. As we *Suspend* we're on a roll, our generativity is in motion. We *Absorb*, we *Connect*, we *Envision*, we *Stream* (the *ACES* creativity model).[4] We become receptive to image streams, analogies, and visual linkages in our minds and give greater *Genuine Voice* to them.

The philosopher Martin Heidegger advised, "We make a space inside ourselves, so that being can speak." Yes, and as we learn to make inner space and hear more from own being, we also make more space from which we can listen to, and hear, other people.

1. Prather, *Notes to Myself.*
2. Bohm, *On Dialogue,* 20–39.
3. Gelb and Caldicott, *Innovate Like Edison,* 91.
4. Carson, *Creative Mind,* Ch. 5–7, 11.

Can we realistically learn to get better at *Suspending*? Is this possible? Yes, it is. We first make it our *intention* to practice *Suspending* more of the time, especially in dialogical conversations where we're wanting to enlarge the diameter and circumference of our thinking. Our progress begins with setting our intention to de-automatize our reactions, to not always react as we habitually have. We consciously want to impede, to interfere with, these automatic and dogmatic dig-in conversational reflexes. We choose to not be an automaton. We seek to awaken ourselves from our automated perceptions, emotions, thoughts, and reactions.[5]

And if our own thoughts, if what we are telling ourselves, is making this seem impossible, we then might choose to put space around this self-limiting self-talk. We can practice *Suspending* the very beliefs and self-suggestions that stop us from *Suspending*, we can lessen our attachment to them.

First, we can remind ourselves of the possibility of *Suspending* by doing the pen-squeezing exercise repeatedly across time, for this exercise works its way into our muscle memory and gives us a directly embodied cognition and feeling of what *Suspending* is about. Our muscle memory provides a bodily-based touchstone experience of what we're to do at the level of consciousness: stop squeezing, ease off, lighten up on our mental grip.

Another way we can move into greater *Suspending* is this: when a thought occurs to us that we want to dis-identify with and be less attached to for now, we can say "I am *having* this thought, but I am *not* this thought." In other words, we mentally and explicitly remind ourselves that just as the sky has clouds passing through it, we have self-limiting thoughts that move through our mind, but our mind is larger than any of these specific thoughts. Little thoughts pass through Big Mind, and we remind ourselves of this with the metaphor of little clouds through Big Sky.

It helps to literally go outside and observe passing clouds and their situation within the vastly larger context of Big Sky to bring home this imagery. Or, for now, look at the ink marks on this page. These have been the focus of your attention. Now shift your focus to the blank page on which these ink marks sit: this is the sky. Breathe it in. Notice the difference this makes? It's about focus, where we choose to place our *focus*.

Another verbal device we can use with ourselves is to say "Now I am *aware* of having this *thought*, but *I am not* this *thought*." This places the bulk of our attention on our *Awareness* through which a self-limiting thought is moving, rather than investing in the details of the thought itself.

5. Tart, *Waking Up*, Ch. 3.

Figure and ground get switched, we change our focus, and this can flip us into greater *Suspending*.

For example, my conversational partner might say something I don't agree with, but instead of stopping at hearing my internal voice say "What a stupid thing to say" I pull back and instead shift my focus to merely witnessing myself having that thought, and loosening my grip on it: "Now I am *aware* of *having* this thought, but *I* am *not* this thought." If we want to, we can even take it to the next step and provide an even greater wedge: "Now I'm *aware* that I'm *aware* I'm having this thought." A slight adjustment of focus: less hot-and-go, more cool and slow.

These mental gymnastics are to distance us from the close-up intricacies of a given thought itself, to zoom-out to a larger view, a wider aperture, and put things in another perspective. We're de-fusing from the control this little thought might have over us, putting our attention not on its substance but by knowing that individual thoughts are passing through our mind constantly, and not all of them (or any?) are *The Entire and Final Truth*. Any single thought is just another thought among the hundreds of thousands that will pass through our mind this week. William James put it well: "The art of being wise is the art of knowing what to overlook."[6] During *Suspending*, we *Over-Look* our thoughts in order to overlook them.

To call upon the de-automatizing power of another metaphor, we can let ourselves know that thoughts, opinions, beliefs, positions, are akin to leaves floating down a stream, and rather than place our mental focus on any given *leaf* for very long, we next switch our focus to *the stream itself* in which the *leaf* is floating by. We mentally practice switching back and forth, leaves and stream. We recognize the transience of mental contents, the leaves, their temporariness, and give larger recognition to the *overall stream of consciousness* through which the contents float along and out of view. This metaphor can work wonders to enable us to put things in perspective, to help us *Suspend* a bit.

In both of the above metaphorical mental models, sky and stream, we reverse what we place in the foreground and background of our awareness. We foreground Big Sky or Big Stream, the larger whole, and put in the background the passing contents we intend to downplay. As for contents, easy come, easy go. Contents are ephemeral; it is our larger and open *Awareness* that remains constant. We decide to place *Awareness* itself, Big Sky or Big Stream, as our focus, not the passing details and debris.

6. James, *Essays and Lectures*.

Another useful metaphor is imagining "turning down the volume" on the clamoring voices in our head that tempt us to stubbornly hold onto, and defend, entrenched positions. It's not that we need to get rid of these voices, we just imagine them coming out of our phone or other sound source further away from where we are and the volume being turned down lower than usual. Muffled background noise, but nothing center-stage. The sounds are lowered, harder to discern, not worth giving much attention to, barely audible white noise.

Also, we can call upon yet another useful and mighty metaphor, the image of ice cubes or blocks of ice representing our frozen opinions or entrenched positions on some topic, and then we visualize these ice cubes or frozen blocks melting, becoming water, soft and fluid and flowy. This transformation from frozen hard ice blocks or cubes to the malleability of water can be useful. Water is a shape-shifter par excellence, highly adaptable and incredibly powerful. At times we ourselves can benefit from mentally thawing out our solidified positions, to let them melt and morph into more freely flowing flexibilities. "Be like water" is ancient timeless wisdom we can draw upon as a mental model to facilitate our transition into *Suspending*.[7] To melt, to de-solidify, to unfreeze, to soften our mental hard edges. We can always refreeze later, if we need to, but for just now, for dialoguing, we can choose to *become like water*.

Yet another powerful metaphor comes from an ancient classic Zen story, one you might be familiar with. Two young scholars, both large of ego and pretentiousness, come to visit a Zen master. They want him to teach them advanced Zen philosophy, though it soon becomes apparent to the master that their extensive book learning and pride has already closed their minds. He asks them if they would like tea, and they say yes. He deliberately fills their cups to overflowing. They shout, "No more will go in." To which the Zen master replies in a doubly meaningful tone of voice, "Your cups already seem to be so full, and will receive no more tea." This was his symbolic way of telling these young scholars they're not yet ready for further learning, their minds are already excessively packed.[8]

This notion of "emptying our cup," making more room for the new to come in, can be another mighty image to internally activate during dialoguing. Our aim in dialoguing is to become open and receptive, and for this to occur we must first "empty our cup." My Seminar in Listening students

7. Chan, *The Way of Lao Tzu*, Ch. 8.
8. Suzuki, *Zen Buddhism*, Ch. 2.

are inevitably struck by this concise and apt ancient metaphor; it has staying power, and sticks with them to call upon as needed as they continue on.

Another ancient East Asian metaphor related to *Suspending* that can be beneficial to draw upon is this one: "You cannot keep birds of sadness from flying over your head. But you can stop them from building a nest in your hair." The first action difficult to take, the other much more possible. Flying by, okay, but no nests. To use a different and related metaphor: fires, when not refueled, go out.

In addition to a metaphorical mindset another main tool we can use to assist us in moving into *Suspending* is, of course, our all-purpose friend breath awareness. Whenever we sense we're holding too tightly onto a position or belief or opinion, at that instant we remember we're *breathing*. More than this, *we feel our breathing in, and our breathing out*, we make nothing in the world more important than *experiencing our body as it is, breathing*. This changes our focus from the thought in our head to the air coming into and out of our lungs, and allows us to step away from getting caught in the quicksand of our counter-productive thoughts.

We feel our midsection or lower chest expand with incoming air, and contract as we breathe out. We feel the air passing through our nostrils and mouth. We feel that precise micro-moment where in-breath all of a sudden turns and becomes out-breath, and vice-versa. Let's practice this right now: breathing in and out once as you *Slow Down*; in and out once again, as you *Stand Back*; in and out once as you *See More*; and in and out, with slow release, as you *Step Forth Wisely*.

Again, somewhere between fifteen to twenty-five thousand times a day we're breathing air in and out, on average (depending upon our personal physiology and activity level), yet we're oblivious to nearly all of these breathings. During breath awareness we grant our breathing process central place. We attend to it, claim it, own it, enjoy it. Our practice of breath awareness is central to our practice of *Suspending*, as well as aiding us in strengthening our focusing skills, and promoting stress reduction and healing.[9]

I have across the years seen dialogue students make tremendous gains in the area of *Suspending*. The pen-squeezing exercise is the catalyst for initially deepening their understanding. Their ongoing breath awareness practice is also a dramatically effective tool in this project. Their repeated recognition that "I *have* thoughts, but *I am not* my thoughts"

9. Goleman, *Focus*, Part II.

takes it further. The metaphors of clouds in the sky, leaves in the stream, turning down the volume, being like water, emptying our cup, these too can handily assist in *Suspending*.

It's our do-it-yourself inside job, fed by choice and intention.

Another verbal device I've used in dialogue seminar is to have students use the word "PO" if they choose to, right before saying anything they think could be heard as "outlandish." By saying "PO" they're meaning that "I'm just saying this to see what it joggles in your mind, to see if it stimulates any images or shadings in your thinking." The "PO" device comes from pioneering creativity specialist Dr. Edward De Bono and is extracted from the words "poetry," "possible," "hypothesis," and "suppose."[10] "PO" is a shorthand device, a simple code word to help us efficiently sidestep logic and reasonability. It asks others to practice their *Suspending*, to cut us some slack and not judge us as we stream forth our words.

Dialoguing isn't a battle of messages, it's a collaborative learning conversation. *Person-centered* inquiry and exploration is our objective. To get there requires *Suspending*. This is a learned skill that we get better at with repeated practice. We practice moving from certainty to curiosity, debate to discovery, evaluation to exploration. We listen expansively from silence at times. We slink between and around our mental categories, and, when all goes well, we tumble into inner spaciousness. We go for wide open spaces, for Big Sky mind, whenever we can allow ourselves this freedom of reach. Our breathing comes in handy for helping this mental widening to happen.

And to enable others to *Suspend* more easily we don't pretend to be speaking *The Absolute and Total Truth*. Instead, we go out of our way to make it clear that we know we're presenting *our own personal truths* about topics, from *our own personal frame of reference*. We speak in a mode of "to-me-ness," making it clear that "Based on what I've been through, this is how it's seeming to me so far, at this point in time, and I grant that not everyone else will be experiencing it this same way."

We learn to stand shoulder-to-shoulder beside each other looking outward and inward and *inquiring together*, rather than facing down one another with certitude, and eliciting defensiveness and counter-attack. We go for the spaces between and around our solid mental categories and positions: for now, we *empty our cup*. And we stay with topics, at least for now, that will enable this; we want to build a strong container before we try to launch into "hot-button" topics.

10. De Bono, *Lateral Thinking*, 246–49.

Dr. Martin Buber once witnessed a dialogical conversation between two of his male friends that eventually turned into a verbal "duel," presumably to impress their female onlookers (or so Buber speculated), and one of these friends "did not speak with his usual composure and strength, but he scintillated, he fought, he triumphed. The dialogue was destroyed."[11] These words of Buber are striking, capturing well the idea that while one might "win" at conversational dueling and impress himself and the on-looking crowd, they simultaneously destroy possibilities for genuine dialogue. A superficial victory, yet at the expense of authentic dialogue.

Buber's story also reminds me of the words of Dr. Robert Hutchins when he wrote that, "Dialogue is the negation of force. We have reached the point, in any event, when force cannot unite the world; it can merely destroy it."[12]

For dialoguing to occur, we need to practice *emptying our cup*.

In ancient Eastern wisdom the *empty cup* remains a strong point of entry. As Grigg expresses it, "Emptiness, therefore, becomes the condition that provides maximum range and perspective, maximum flexibility and freedom to move and respond."[13] The more that dialogue participants tone-down their rigid position statements, strong semantics, and nonverbal cues of negative judgment, the less they'll alienate others and the more room everyone will have in which to move around, and feel and follow the free flow of dialoguing.

If genuine dialoguing is to happen everyone needs to lighten-up on their stranglehold grips on their stances and styles. Our often dysfunctional "go-to" communication routines need to be placed on hold. We accept our defensiveness as predictable, normal, and generic, and then drop out of it. Gliding into defenselessness becomes our strength, and saves the day. We back off on our mental tensions and invite, for purposes of dialoguing, "don't know" mind, and remain connected with our "center" in the midst of conditions.[14]

Time for an upgrade to *Suspending*.

To help get us there, we feel our *breathing* in and out, in and out, in and out, and in and out, as we *Slow Down*, and *Stand Back*, and *See More*,

---

11. Buber, "Elements of the Inter-human," 359–60.

12. Matson and Montagu, *Human Dialogue*, vi.

13. Grigg, *The Tao of Zen*, 234.

14. Wilhelm and Jung, *Golden Flower*, 34–56.

and then *Step Forth Wisely*. This takes only seconds, and provides us transition into *Suspending*. We back in, gently.

Taking Action

It's time to work with metaphors of Big Sky and of "being like water" in your mind, and the "emptying our cup," and with our breathing, so we can know what *Suspending* is about. We'll also want to do the pen-squeezing exercise again and again.

We let this thought percolate: at times, by our choice, we can temporarily relax our stranglehold grip on those beliefs and positions that we hold as *The Unassailable Truth*. It doesn't mean that we're abandoning these positions forever, but only for the moment. We can of course return to these positions and to a strong grip later on, as we choose. For the sake of dialogue, though, everyone has to lighten up at least little if we're to get off the ground and become airborne.

Practice saying "Now I'm aware that I'm having this thought, but I am not this thought" instead of identifying with the content of the passing thought itself. And while listening to others with views different from yours, take four slow and unobtrusive breaths in and out, each time silently repeating to yourself, "Breathing in, I intend *Suspending*. Breathing out, I let go of tight grip."

Reflecting

In the same way I see others sometimes clinging too stubbornly to their beliefs and opinions, I can imagine that I at times cling overly tightly to my own. I can understand that for exploratory dialoguing to occur, taking a time-out from my attachment to my positions, and others doing the same, can give us room to roam around together, exploring lively worlds of story, idea, and imagination. We can always return to familiar positions when our dialoguing is complete, up to us. But to give dialogue a fair chance, Suspending is what I choose to start to practice, and I also encourage my dialogue partners to aim for the same.

13

Behind the Curtain:
Dialogue Principles

THE LATE DAVID BOHM was a professor of theoretical physics at the University of London. He is especially well known for his contributions to quantum physics, and to the study and practice of human dialogue, a seemingly strange combination of interests at first glance, but maybe not so after all. Along with Dr. Martin Buber and Dr. Carl Rogers, Dr. Bohm is one of the godfathers of contemporary dialogue studies and practice. Bohm was a colleague and friend of Einstein and other bright peers.

Dr. Bohm saw dialogue to be "the free play of ideas" with no particular pre-planned destination or outcome in mind, and with ample *Suspending* all along the way: "Dialogue can be considered as a free flow of meaning between people in communication, in the sense that a stream flows between banks."[1] Bohm spoke of four major overlapping principles that he believed undergird human dialogue, standing silently beneath our up-top dialogue practices. These four principles underlying dialogue's "free play of ideas" are briefly summarized here. You might want to know about them, for they hover in the background of our **WEG-VIBES** practices, quietly behind the scenes.[2]

The Principle of Dynamic Process recognizes that "life is a verb," that life is a multitude of processes that are constantly in motion, in dynamic flux, and that not much stays static and immobile for long. All is flowing, morphing, changing, evolving. We're back to Heraclitus and his ancient observation that we can't step in the same river twice, for already by the second stepping the river won't be exactly the same, nor will we: "The only thing that is constant is change." Everything is moving, vibrating, patterning, altering, alternating, even when it might not look that way on the surface.

1. Bohm, see https://www.bohmdialogue.org.
2. Bohm, *On Dialogue*; also see Isaacs, *Dialogue*, Ch. 2, 4–7.

Knowing this is dependent upon our perceptual vantage-point; sometimes we can't notice the momentum of it all because of where we're standing in the situation. If we had microscopic vision, we could see the underlying momentum, but we don't have, yet we've been around long enough by now to know that change happens.

This *Principle of Dynamic Process* gives us hope when our dialogue seems stifled, stuck, stalled, encouraging us not to succumb to dismay since, in time, fixity will yield to movement. This principle keeps us alert, adaptable, flexible. Flux is the order of the day, so we stay alert, conscious, aware, nimble. We practice patience, for all is in motion, even when it appears not to be the case from where we're standing. We return to faith, knowing this too shall pass.

The Principle of Wholeness reminds us that from close-up viewings we often see only disconnected details, isolated objects, random puzzle pieces. Bohm points out that we fragment the world with our minds, dividing the *Whole* into pieces, slicing it and dicing it, and then our mind forgets we've done this. We smash the world into chunks, analyze the chunks, and fail to remember the *Whole*.

But when we stand back and look at the "bigger picture" we can witness more continuity, cohesiveness, and *Wholeness* than we've remembered. This *Principle of Wholeness* reminds us to pull back from our zoomed-in close-ups and zoom-out to longer-shots as well, to take-in more of the grand context, the larger scene, and gain overall perspective.

With patience and distance comes enlarged vision. We breathe in and out now, as we *Slow Down*; we take in a second breath as we *Stand Back*, and then we exhale it; we take in, and then let out, a third breath, as we make ourselves available to *See More*; and finally we take a fourth breath in, and out, and *Step Forth Wisely*.

Zen teacher Thich Nhat Hanh is illustrating the *Principle of Wholeness* (along with our next principle as well) when he points out that in the blank sheet of white paper in our printer there is also the tree from which the paper came, the earth in which the tree grew, the sun and rain that nourished the tree, the lumberjack who cut tree, the logger who hauled it in a truck, the mill that processed the wood pulp into paper, the store that distributed it, and so much more, including us, as we look at the paper with our eyes and brain. Hahn speaks of "inter-being," meaning an inter-connectedness of elements within a larger hidden system that often eludes detection upon superficial glance.[3]

The "eye of the artist" sees not just the isolated elements, the individual parts, but how the various parts end-up fitting together into a more complete landscape. In dialogue we can slow down and practice looking with the "eye of the artist," gaining distance, seeing how slivers and shards fit into overall patterns. Everything is more inter-dependent, systemically related, than it could seem at casual close-up glimpse from our limited vantage point.

At times it's our self-chosen silence that enables us to attain this enhanced perspective. *Empathy* too can provide this expanded vantage point, and, of course, *Suspending* can bring renewed comprehension of a grander *Whole*. There's always more to see, and more inter-connection than we tend to realize. Our frame of mind at times needs to be made larger. As brain scientist Richard Davidson has put it, "The capacity to remain with your attention open in a panoramic awareness lets you attend with equanimity, without getting caught in a bottom-up capture that ensnares the mind in judging and reactivity . . . "[4]

Another way we can see more of the *Whole* in dialogue is to understand that we meet in a third space: Dr. Buber called it "the Between." This is the ridge where *"I"* and *"Thou"* commune. In dyadic dialogue (two people) for example, there is one person, and another, and the "chemical" conjunction of the two. For example, there is Bryan, there is Ron, and there is "Ron-Bryan" (or "Bryan-Ron"). This entity, this joint pairing, is a singular phenomenon in this world, and not equivalent to "Tori-Bryan," "Bryan-John," "Kiana-Ron," or any other pairing interface. On the entire planet, only "Bryan-Ron" is the "Bryan-Ron" thing.

At moments in dialogue we come to palpably know this, we sense the unique distinctive confluence of persons within our pairing or group, and this awakens us to more of the *Whole*. Standing back from the individual trees we're comprehending the larger forest of which they're a part. To use another metaphor, we see not only five separate fingers but the entire hand, wrist, forearm, arm, and body of which they are a part.

The Principle of Participation maintains that we're not so separate and divided from the world as it can at times appear, and that "*I am in the world, and the world is in me.*" There are a multitude of ways that "the world

---

3. Hanh, *Peace is Every Step*, 95-96.
4. See Goleman, *Focus*, 55.

is within us." At some level, for instance, we feel that people we've known and loved are here within us in memory and mind, even when not bodily present. We know that our worlds of perception and knowledge are heavily influenced by these personal relationships, and by the cultural institutions and other membership and reference groups in which we've been embedded: "I am in the world, and the world is in me."

Also, at moments with mother nature we can feel swept up into warm breezes and swaying trees, the colors and sounds and moods and tones of nature, and feel at one with it all: "I am in nature, and nature is in me." The *Principle of Participation* can help in reconnecting us with the natural world in which we live and move and have our being, a reminder to return to ecological *Empathy*.[5] Bohm says that our mind stands between us and all that is, like a thick border wall. With the *Principle of Participation* we consciously reclaim our convergence with the rest of what is.

There's also what the famous astronomer Dr. Carl Sagan pointed out to us: "The nitrogen contained in our genes, the calcium in our blood and the carbon in our apple pie were made in the cosmic kitchen that is the star. Our bodies are made up of the particles that constitute the stars. Indeed, in a very profound sense, we are children of the stars."[6] Sagan here is saying that "I am in the universe, and the universe is in me."

But I think one of the understandings that most brought this principle home to me personally was grasping the fact that human cells in our bodies are vastly outnumbered by the microbial cells that are everywhere on our skin and eyeballs and in our nose and ears and intestines (a hundred trillion microorganisms in our guts alone).[7] In sum, there are at least *ten times* more *microbial* cells within each of us than *human* cells: "*I am in the world, and the world is in me.*"

Then when we reflect on the fact that the human brain, heart, liver, and kidneys are each between 65 percent and 85 percent water (with the adult human body around 60 percent water overall), and understand that *our water molecules aren't human*, this too drives home the point that "*the world is in me.*" Add to this the knowledge that most of our DNA is shared with other animals: we have 88 percent shared genes with mice, 84 percent shared with dogs and horses, 47 percent shared with fruit flies, 24

---

5. Abram, *Becoming Animal*.

6. Sagan, *Cosmos*, Preface.

7. Achenbach, "Growing on You," 19.

percent shared with rice, and 24 percent with wine grapes![8] The bottom-line is that it's literally true that the overwhelming majority of our cells and genetic information is not specifically human: "*I am in the world, and the world is in me.*"

If this all weren't enough, add the one quadrillion Argon atoms we're breathing in at this very second that have been breathed in and out by other contemporary humans all around this world. Then add another million Argon atoms we're breathing in and out right now that were breathed by our human ancestors, dinosaurs, and a multitude of other living creatures across the millennia.[9] It is, again, literally accurate to announce that "*I am in the world, and the world is in me.*"

To consciously *Participate* in more of this *Whole*, we breathe in, and out, and *Slow Down*; and then we take another breath in, and out as we internally *Stand Back*; and then we breathe in and out again, as we appreciatively *See More*; we're then ready to breathe again, in and out, and to *Step Forth Wisely.*

During dialoguing, reminding ourselves of the *Principle of Participation* helps us to "listen as if it's all in me," that no matter what gets said or who feels what, "This, too, is in me." This *Principle of Participation* is an *Empathy*-builder extraordinaire. As the significant sociologists Berger and Luckman once phrased it, "We not only live in the same world, we participate in each other's being."[10]

I personally first invoke the *Principle of Wholeness* to remind myself that everything "out there" is more interconnected with itself than superficial glance reveals, and then I draw upon the *Principle of Participation* to prompt myself to recall that the "out there" is in fact not as separate from me as my mind would often have me think it is. This gives pause, enlarges vision, and reduces the illusion of separation.

In our ongoing dialoguing, we may indirectly and directly uncover other ways that this bountiful principle also has truth, meaning, value, and application.

The Principle of Unfolding comes from Bohm's understanding of physics, as do all of our four principles. It holds that there is both an invisible ("implicate") order and a visible ("explicate") order, and that what we see and

8. Zimmer, "Genes Are Us," 102–03.

9. Gordon, *Tuning-In*, 302–05.

10. Berger and Luckman, *Social Construction of Reality*, Ch. 1.

experience on the visible or explicate level comes out of the implicate order. Things "unfold" into our world and take shape as *something*.

Not only does this happen at the level of physics, however. Bohm suggests that from the implicate order we in dialogue can learn to bring insights and ideas into being, we can *unfold* new creation into the world from the invisible implicate order. We ourselves can become authentic seers and speakers as we find our voices and become as the seed is to the tree, the aperture, the opening through which beautiful contribution can be released.[11]

When I think of this *Principle of Unfolding* I am reminded of the luminaries within the arts, and philosophy, and the sciences who across the centuries have spoken of the creative spirit, the force of inspiration upon which they've drawn to bring their work into tangible form. The list is vast: Tchaikovsky, Nietzsche, Wordsworth, Browning, Shelley, Wagner, Tolstoy, Carlyle, Voltaire, Coleridge, Balzac, Schelling, Chopin, Proust, and on it goes.

In all fields of human thought, invention, and creativity, testimony to the powers of "inspiration" or "intuition" or what Dr. Pitirim Sorokin of Harvard called "supra-consciousness" abound.[12] Speaking here on the creative spirit is the great composer Mozart: "What, you ask, is my method in writing and elaborating my large and lumbering things? I can, in fact, say nothing more about it than this: I do not know myself and can never find out. When I am in a particularly good condition, then the thoughts come to me in a rush, and best of all. Whence and how I do not know, and cannot learn."[13]

And here is the brilliant existential philosopher, Nietzsche: " . . . one becomes nothing but a medium for super-mighty influences. That which happens can only be termed revelation; that is to say, that suddenly, with unutterable certainty and delicacy, something becomes visible and audible and shakes and rends one to the depths of one's being. One hears, one does not seek; one takes, one does not ask who it is that gives; like lightning a thought flashes out, of necessity, in complete form . . . "[14]

In such moments of *unfolding* from the implicate level to the explicate order there is no strenuous effort of ego; on the contrary, there is a

11. Bohm, *On Creativity*, Ch. 5.

12. Sorokin, *Ways and Power of Love*, Ch. 8.

13. Sorokin, *Ways and Power*, 106.

14. Sorokin, *Ways and Power*, 106.

self-forgetting, and the artist or inventor or composer or writer or mathematician or scientist becomes a suitable channel through which content then flashes forth and streams out into the world.

This is what human dialoguing, too, can be about at times, where each participant in the conversation trusts the larger *Whole* and has deep-seated faith in the *Principle of Unfolding*. When each person surrenders to whatever forces there are in the universe of creative discourse that inspire and infuse receptive human beings, they can become portals through which *unfolding* manifests. *Generative* dialoguing at its finest opens the way for the operation of the *Principle of Unfolding*.

This has been a quick intro to four of the chief principles that Dr. David Bohm believed to be relevant to, and that can infuse, the human dialogue process. It could be said that our **WEG-VIBES** practices are permeated by these principles. Remembering these four principles of *Dynamic Process*, *Wholeness*, *Participation*, and *Unfolding* can enlarge and enhance our frame for reflection, budging us into both grander outlook and more penetrating comprehension.

To dialogue about how this might be true in any given instance is tantalizing, as is speculating as to what principles might be driving which practices, and when, and how. Here itself is bountiful material for dialoguing, and for breathing our way into.

Taking Action

Think about these four principles: *Dynamic Process*, *Wholeness*, *Participation*, and *Unfolding*. How do you, at first glance, imagine these principles could inform and inflect your dialogue practice? Any images or thoughts come to you right away? Whether yes or no, do let these principles linger in the background, hovering, a gauzy scrim, a backdrop that suddenly illuminates at times to allow deeper visioning. And notice how these principles relate to your daily life in general.

Through dark glasses and with soft eyes return to gazing upon these four dialogue principles now and again using Principle-Vision, and see what they enable you to discern.

Reflecting

Which of these principles am I especially drawn to: Dynamic Motion, Wholeness, Participation, or Unfolding? What about them calls out to me? How do these principles fit in with my life? How do they feel familiar? Strange?

Someday, when the time is auspicious, can I begin to think about which **WEG-VIBES** *practices might stem from, or relate to, which principles? And can I let whatever power I find in these principles gradually guide me as I walk the way of dialogue?*

14

The Call to Wonder:
Star-Bursting

IT'S HELPFUL BEFORE BEGINNING any attempt at dialoguing to let everyone know of the **WEG-VIBES** guidelines. Make these public and try to have them in writing. Maybe photocopy and distribute the chapter on "Our Dialogue Model: **WEG-VIBES**," plus the observation form located at the end of this volume. List them on the board, or anywhere else they can be readily seen throughout the dialogue. Here's what to return to striving toward, again and again.

Let participants know that the fewer the **WEG-VIBES** practices that get enacted and sustained, the lower the probability of their getting to creative dialoguing. The more of these practices that folks are respecting and consistently putting into practice, the more dialogical they're becoming.

Becoming aware of how we're doing in the **WEG-VIBES** practices is a continuously recurring process. We talk topic and we forget our process, then we regain awareness of **WEG-VIBES** and we almost subliminally reflect on how we're doing, then we adjust accordingly, and we continue on. And we repeat as often as needed, and repetition of this cycle *will* be needed.

If people want to supplement **WEG-VIBES** with any additional guidelines, dialogue about this too, and go with group sentiment in each case.

One of my favorite methods both for instilling a dialogical frame of mind and also for coming up with eventual dialogue topics is what has been called "mining for questions"[1] or "*Star-Bursting*."[2] This question-generation activity usually takes from ten to thirty minutes, depending upon the number of participants. First, we pick a topic. Next, instead of giving our beliefs and opinions on this topic we're going to specialize solely in pouring forth questions pertaining to our topic for our pre-designated

1. Isaacs, *Dialogue*, 148–50.
2. Kirby and Goodpaster, *Thinking*, 104–05.

amount of time. We raise questions, without ever trying to answer even a single one of them. We're not about answers for now, we're exclusively about questions.

For instance, if the topic we choose is "love" and we're in a group of a dozen or more people, we might give ourselves thirty minutes to come up with as many questions pertaining to "love" as we possibly can. If there are only two of us in this interactive dialoguing, then ten minutes on the clock could be enough time. If there are four or five us, fifteen to twenty minutes might do. But I hasten to add that the real treat comes by *Star-Bursting* for half an hour, and I do encourage you at some point in your dialogue journey to proceed for this long in a group setting.

To get our *Star-Bursting* underway, we set a timer, and set this rule: *all we can do in our allotted time is generate questions; we're not out to even start to try to answer any of them.* Maybe later, another time, but not now.

Nor are we judging the *quality* of each question, or we'll get bogged down. We're solely going for *quantity* of contributions. We're simply letting questions pop into our mind, and *Genuinely Voicing* them as soon as they burst into our brain. We forget censoring, we skip editing. We focus only on getting questions *out there*. We're not out to judge or reply to them, but to *release* them into the world, to *Genuinely Voice* them, to *Star-Burst* them.

We completely abandon all effort to *answer* anything: *we create questions, and that's all.* Ideally, we'll have a person or two jotting these questions down, keeping track of what we come up with. We exercise patience all along the way, and we receptively relax into the silences, waiting until more questions come. And we strive for *Equality of Participation* and not a minority of us generating a majority of our questions. Spaces will need to be made at points along the way for quieter persons to enter the flow. These persons should not be repeatedly crowded out by faster thinkers and speakers.

One person's question will stimulate other peoples' minds to come up with yet other questions, each of us influencing our other dialogue partners by the doors and windows we open through the questions we create. We bounce off one another's queries, we piggyback, we become kindly contrarian, we do whatever it takes to let the questions keep flowing forth. We begin haltingly at first, but across time our momentum accelerates: "What is love, anyway?" "Is there even such a thing as love?" "Is love an illusion?" "What's the value of love to human survival?" "How many layers or dimensions does love have?" "How many different flavors of love are there?" "What is it that all the various types of love have in common?" "What does it mean to say that love never dies, that it's eternal?" "Why is it so hard to love our enemies?" "Is it realistic to think that we can ever learn to love any of our enemies?" "Why would we want to ever do that?" "Can we learn to love better across a lifetime?" "What would it require to make progress in learning the art of love?" "What does it mean to say that love even transcends death?" "Is love all in the brain?" "How much truth is there in the line that says 'Whatever the question, love is the answer'?" "Is hate the true opposite of love?" "Are love and 'power' enemies?" "How subject is love to scientific analysis?" "What more is love than a need?" "How are love, divinity, and humanity related?"

It's absolutely amazing how a half hour of reaching for questions in our topic area, without trying to answer any of them, fills our mind with wonderment. No longer preoccupied with answer-getting we become enthralled and overtaken by the sheer spirit of curiosity. After as long as thirty minutes of *Star-Bursting* our mind might not even want to proffer an answer to any of the questions we've come up with, not today anyway, for answers by now can seem so small and confining. Even if we were to try to offer answers, we would see that each attempted answer invites an even better next question.

Our mind has perhaps become enlarged past seeking answers and in-stead plunged far into the interrogative mode rather than the reductive and declarative. We feel refreshingly inquisitive and outward-looking. We're not wanting to close-down, we're eager to continue wandering and wondering. At this stage we're not reduced to *advocacy* but basking in the afterglow of having catapulted ourselves into elongated *exploratory inquiry*. Our minds have awakened and our consciousness is broader than, say, half an hour ago. *Inquiry* has become its own intrinsically pleasing reward.

Now is the time to breathe in and out, as we *Slow Down*; and now to slowly breathe in and out as we *Stand Back*; and next to inhale and exhale our way into *Seeing More*; and finally to inhale and exhale once more, as we *Step Forth Wisely* into reflection.

At our next gathering we can venture speculative and tentative partial responses to one or more of our generated questions if we so choose, but maybe for right now it's best to simply let it rest and enjoy the results of this experience, one we've never had before! Think of it: when in your life have you ever come up with one question after another for twenty minutes or half an hour straight, and with no attempted answers? Probably not often, and most likely never.

Together, collaboratively, we've cast open the doors of inquiry. Let us celebrate what we've just brought to pass, and not too quickly leave this special mood behind. May we bask awhile in the afterglow of sustained inquiry.

As Dr. Carl Jung warned, "The more that critical reason dominates, the more impoverished life becomes."[3] The critical mind and the creative mind, we need both: goodbye domination, welcome balance. Generating good questions that are then lived-into across time can be more important and valuable than quick and facile answers that are prematurely advocated. And as Nobel Prize-winning theoretical physicist Richard Feynman went on to say, "I would rather have questions that can't be answered than answers that can't be questioned."[4]

The *Star-Bursting* (or "mining for questions") method offered here is a wise place for any dialogue group to begin from, and remains a personal favorite of mine. Reaching for questions is a fertile way to emerge with questions for future dialogues, but more than this it's an experience in and of itself that dramatically illustrates the compelling beauty of the interrogative mode, which is the underlying mode and theme of dialogue: shared *inquiry*.

At some point with a dialogue group please do spend thirty minutes exclusively *Star-Bursting* questions, and, at least for the time being, forget about pursuing answers. Leave even partial responses for the morrow, and today bathe in the pools of wonder you together create.

We've gone from a narrowing down > to an opening out <, and this can deliver us into an incredible spirit of dialogical potentiality.

When Carl Rogers and Martin Buber held a public dialogue at the University of Michigan years ago, Dr. Rogers prepared nine preliminary questions for a what was to be a one-hour dialogue. He and Buber were only able to get to four of the prepared questions, and that took an hour and a half.[5] Good questions lead us to places (including to yet other questions) that we don't anticipate, and are luxurious entryways to *shared inquiry*.

---

3. Jung, *Memories, Dreams, Reflections*, Prologue.

4. Feynman, AZQuotes.com.

5. Cissna and Anderson, "Theorizing About Dialogic Moments," 95–6.

Taking Action

We often prioritize answer-giving over the development of truly good questions. It's time, at last, to become more acquainted with the pleasures that arrive with forming provocative and evocative questions. Answers are a dime a dozen, *advocacy* is cheap and plentiful. Unveiling groundbreaking questions is a far higher art. Catch a glimpse of what could be asked. Bring to light that which has not already, for you, been a completed item of *inquiry*. Unmask superficial answers and plumb down to unasked questions that lay beneath. Catch sight of what hasn't been seen; scout out the unknown, light up the night sky with *Star-Bursting*.

Or, switching metaphors, embark on an excavation to mine for questions, and see if you strike gold. This week ask a friend or family member or your partner to *Star-Burst* with you, even if only for five minutes. Pick a topic area, set a timer, and begin. Chances are, you will catch and ride *the spirit of inquiry*, and this is to advance on the way of dialogue.

Reflecting

Is it possible that in the past I haven't wondered enough? Maybe I've been so busy looking around for answers that I've lost touch with finding worthwhile questions in the first place. With a transition from answering to asking, maybe I can rock my (the?) world. Coming up with edgy, provocative, profound questions, and living into some of them for a while, might be a wiser use of my mental powers.

What if I go less often for a "period" and more often for a "question mark"? Is this likely to narrow or widen my consciousness? How about if I give a green light to getting swept up in the spirit of dialogical inquiry, becoming more about raising intriguing questions than delivering stock answers?

15

Check-Ins, Go-Arounds, and Quotations

I AIM FOR DIALOGUE at each and every class session in all my university communication classes. I'm not out to hold debates or to pursue problem-solving group discussions, but to have open-ended dialogues on topics relevant to that given day's assigned readings. We're aiming not for this > but for this <.

It's not as if no advocacy attempts at all will arise, inevitably they will. But we don't emphasize these, dwell on them, feed them in any sustained fashion, not when our aim is dialogue. Our theme is to healthily and curiously *inquire* together, not to get derailed into debate.

How to start a dialogue session? "Check-ins" are often a fine place to begin to loosen-up people for dialogue. I frequently begin my dialogue seminar sessions this way, asking everyone present to take a minute or two and summarize for us the "reality" they're coming in from so far this week, and how they're doing. We have a "go-around," each person in sequence around our circle sharing in turn.

Or, if more than a dozen folks are present and this check-in would take too long, we can simply ask how everyone's "mood" is today, their overall "state of mind" at this point in time, and to briefly speak to this topic for about a minute each. This isn't therapy, it's a check-in.

Other times I might start a session by asking participants to think of, and share with us, any single word that best summarize where they're "at" on this day as our session begins. This takes less clock time than the above methods, gives quick useful feedback to the facilitator, and swiftly focuses group attention. It gets us going.

The above opening check-ins efficiently get people on the same page, even when their responses vary widely, and sometimes give us leads to follow-up on later, or topics to pursue now. Check-ins serve to transition us from our busy day, our phones, our distracted minds, and move more into *Being Now* and *Here* with these other specific persons in this room at this time, and developing a common focus.

They bring us into this physical space, here, now, together, where we can at last *Slow Down* and breathe; where we can *Stand Back*, and take delight in our inhaling and our exhaling; as we next breathe our way into *Seeing More* when we breathe in, and then out; and, finally, we can then breathe, and relax, into *Stepping Forth Wisely*.

Most often I call upon pre-assigned readings as our evocative object for dialogue. I typically put this question, or a variant of it, to the class entire: "Will someone start us off by jumping us into any idea or concept or sentence in today's reading that has significant meaning for you? Something you connected with: it spoke to you, it impacted you, it triggered something within you. What might that be?"

Sometimes I'll call upon specific persons to respond, or simply let the question stand before the group entire. Either way, the intention is to have everyone participate by the end of the session. This can entail being patient during long silences, combined with inviting quieter folks forward by name, along with gently quieting down the most attention-seeking members of the group.

As people begin to respond to the open-ended invitation to address anything of value in the day's reading, I attempt to model the **WEG-VIBES** practices as best I can at that given session, and periodically encourage other dialogue members to do the same.

Or, I might begin by reading aloud a quote from the assigned readings that I especially liked, to link us up with our day's material. For example, in my communication and leadership course one of the books I use is authored by legendary basketball coach Phil Jackson, in which he presents his leadership philosophy for building highly effective teams.[1] So I might get us in motion by sharing something that I found exciting that Phil Jackson wrote, and then see where the dialogue goes from there. I tend to be an enthusiastic reader and responder, and this can be energizing and contagious for contributors to follow.

Or, I might put the students in pairs or small groups and have something like the following printed-out for students to read: "Phil Jackson talks about creating a 'sacred space' for his team, a physical 'holy sanctuary' where they can be reminded that they are on a 'sacred quest.' Have you ever had

---

1. Jackson and Delehanty, *Sacred Hoops*, Ch. 1.

such a physical space at any time in your life, or known anyone who has? If so, talk about this. And if not, can you recall and talk about any physical space that was in any way especially inspiring to you, and how so?"

Here's another item used at that same two-hour-plus session: "Phil Jackson talks about the kind of team or group where 'the strength of the wolf is the pack,' where there is a thinking and moving as 'one,' a heightened group consciousness, a surrender of self-interest, a movement from 'me' to 'we.' Explore together whether you've ever been a member of a group or unit where this degree of unity and synchrony was achieved, and what this was like."[2] This would most often be done in pairs, but can also work in small groups.

Also at that same session I had us respond to these words of Phil Jackson: "The trick is to experience each moment with a clear mind and an open heart. When you do that, the game – and life – will take care of itself."[3] I asked the folks in the class, "What times in your life have you been able to do this? Do you at moments lapse into this 'clear mind and open heart' state currently? If so, when, where, with whom, and how, and what's it like, and what do you wonder about it?"

Same class session, one more from coach: "Phil Jackson says that a great team needs an 'unshakeable desire to win.' He was worried, before Michael Jordan returned to the team, that the players had gotten comfortable with mediocrity.[4] Share a time from your life when you settled for mediocrity, and then a different time when you had a burning desire to achieve something great. Explore the differences."

Openings such as these can lead us into all kinds of places and spaces, whether in pairs, small groups, or in a whole-group circle. Students are self-disclosing about their own personal lives, getting to know one another, building community, and engaging subject content, all at the same time. And things that will be said that can give rise to questions and topics for further probing later on.

I might wrap-up a session such as this one by having us sit in our large class circle again and asking, "How does 'leadership' relate to what happened in your pairings or small group tonight? Was there a 'leader,' or no 'leader,' or two or three 'leaders,' or what? Let's inquire into this for a while, and what we're using this word 'leader' to mean here." Dialogical inquiry

2. Jackson and Delehanty, *Sacred Hoops*, Ch. 1–2.

3. Jackson and Delehanty, *Sacred Hoops*, Ch. 3.

4. Jackson and Delehanty. *Sacred Hoops*, Ch. 11.

is underway, with nobody to be made wrong, and no single answer to be sought. To me this is what learning is about: *inquiring together* <.

In everyday life, of course, dialogue topics tend to grow out of casual conversation naturally. Often, we'll be talking and all of a sudden I find I'm at a *choice-point*: you've said something that I can disagree with and *Defend* against, and maybe debate you about, *or* I can *Suspend* my initial internal reaction and begin to more open-endedly explore this topic area with you. Imagine I pause as I breathe in and out, while I *Stand Back, Slow Down, See More*, and then *Step Forth Wisely*. You as a result aren't placed on the *defensive*, and now we can experiment with *inquiring together*. We can *inquire* into our topic and develop it together, as we practice our **WEG-VIBES** all along our way, and we're doing exactly what it takes to have our conversation become dialogical.

But in more structured large group situations in a time-limited context, preparing to set the stage for *shared inquiry* can be useful, and check-ins, go-arounds, and responding to potent quotations can be especially great pathways to jump-starting dialogue. Let's briefly consider these methods.

Powerful quotations are amassed energy, waiting to be tapped. I can envision contexts, for instance, in which this quote by Omar Bradley, America's last 5-Star General, which I found just this week, could be an efficient intro to a substantial dialogue: "Ours is a world of nuclear giants and ethical infants. If we continue to develop our technology without wisdom or prudence, our servant may prove to be our executioner."[5] We could read this quotation aloud, and then extend this invitation: "Let's dialogue about *technology, ethics*, and *wisdom*, and any connections we see among these, and any related thoughts or apprehensions we might have. We're *not* out to persuade, but to *explore together* our thinking, issues, and concerns."

Another short quote rich with potential: W.H. Auden said, "We must all love one another or die."[6] We might ask, "How is this true for you personally, and for our world, as you see it? What do you personally believe stops us from loving our fellow human beings? Does love, anywhere, ever prevail over division and hostility? As you see it, can this ever happen worldwide? What do you hope?"

E.F. Schumacher believed that "More education can help us only if it produces more wisdom."[7] We could read this quote aloud, and then ask

5. Bradley, AZQuotes.com.
6. Auden, AZQuotes.com.
7. Schumacher, AZQuotes.com.

"What comes to your mind when you think of 'wisdom'? How do you think 'wisdom' might be harder to come by than 'knowledge'? When do you think 'knowledge' has a chance to become 'wisdom'? Who is the wisest human you've ever personally known, and what made them seem so 'wise'? And what else can we wonder about 'wisdom' together?"

Or we can paraphrase quotations that dimly linger within our memory: "Rilke has said that great books make us realize we must change our life. Briefly talk about a book that you've read that's had an impact on how you live your life."

Another paraphrased reference: "In his classic book *Man's Search for Meaning*, Dr. Viktor Frankl says that most people have a 'will to *meaning*,' that there's motivation within each of us to find *meaning* in our life.[8] How and where have you sought for *meaning* in your lifetime? What have you observed and learned along the way?"

Or, anonymously, "It has been said that 'fear is the mother of the event.' Let's talk about how our fears can bring into existence the very things that are feared: how has that even been true for us personally, and how do we also see this formula working in the larger world?"

I love quotations: they persevere because of the pithy and potent manner in which they communicate something important, and they offer a wonderful way to get dialogue up and moving. Anything can become grist for dialogue, as long as it is tenderly treated with the elements of **WEG-VIBES** and as long as *shared inquiry* is our aim.

I hasten to add that in my dialogue seminars and other university classes I choose not to have students encounter explosive "hot-button" topics in too frontal a manner. Why not? The latest National College Health Assessment shows that over 80 percent of students feel emotionally "overwhelmed" at times, over 50 percent feel "hopeless," over 40 percent occasionally feel so depressed that it's hard for them to function, two-thirds often feel quite sad, and about a third are coping with chronic anxiety issues.[9]

In the context of these and related contemporary realities dialogue topics need to be chosen and worded in a manner where they'll not further add to peoples' burdens, but will hopefully help release some of the heavy emotional loads they're already carrying. At least this is how I personally

8. Frankl, *Man's Search for Meaning*.

9. American College Health Association, *National College Health Assessment Report 2019*.

have approached topic selection and wording, inviting dialogue participants to self-disclose, connect, trust, bond, uplift, and to an extent heal as
a result of their participation in our humane dialogue community. Once
strong dialogue containers have been constructed with the WEG-VIBES
practices, advanced challenges can perhaps be undertaken. For now, building bridges is our priority: bridges to self, bridges to other.

Taking Action

Begin to watch how especially good dialogical conversations get going.
Whether in media interviews, in the coffee shop, at work or school, on
podcasts, in living rooms, in the streets, wherever, what's conducive dialogue? How do people get comfortable with each other, and then how do
they actually launch into shared inquiry? How do they avoid getting stuck
in the quicksand of *Defending*, and instead dance into *Suspending*, thereby
allowing dialogue to proceed? Do you see most of the **WEG-VIBES** in
action, or are some not there? What's present in these dialogues, and what
tends to be in short supply? Learn whatever you can about good and poor
choice-making by looking and listening at conversations all around you
in your everyday life.

And how about starting to be on the hunt for good quotations and
writing them down or snapping photos of them so you have stimulating
materials readily at hand when conversing with others? What's the most interesting idea you've heard today, the most intriguing word, the most captivating analogy, the most dramatic statistic, the catchiest example, the most
touching story? Start to jot down and collect these tidbits, become an eager
collector, for these can become doorways to dialogue. Notice what some of
them prompt you to wonder; questions that take loosely take shape, and
percolate within.

Reflecting

*I become excited by ever-present possibilities for dialogue. There is so much to
inquire into, and I can see how presumptuous it is to think that we should have
an opinion and position on everything. I become more modest and humble in
my knowledge claims, and decide to pursue the way of shared inquiry.*

*I realize that I don't need to pretend to have the answers. Socrates was
only considered wise once he admitted to himself and the world that he didn't*

know so much after all, nor did anyone else. He specialized in asking really good questions, and we remember him for this twenty-five centuries later! Humility and wisdom are spun of common cloth, and this is increasingly my garment of choice.

16

"Talk About,"
Sentence-Completions,
and Haiku

BELOW ARE OTHER INVITATIONS I've used in various of my communication classes, all to stimulate dialogical conversation. You'll notice that my favorite opening wording, uttered with supportive vocal intonation, is "*Talk about . . .*" This semantic preface is highly welcoming and open-ended.

If we ask people questions with closed-ended prefaces, we unnecessarily channelize their responses: "Do you think that . . ." "Why did you . . .?" "Is it true that . . .?" "When was . . .?" "How is it possible that . . . ?" These put the other in a somewhat confining position, but "*Tell me about . . .*" or "*Talk about . . .*" or "*Will you talk about . . .*" or "*We'd like to hear you talk about . . .*" can flare us out into wider-latitude open-space regions, they call forth more robust responsiveness.

Or we might instead choose to say "*Help us understand* the history of your views on (e.g., politics), where you think they've come from, and changes in them across your life" (applicable to diverse topics). This too is a useful phrasing, especially in more controversial topic areas.

Up to you exactly how you word your invites, but here are some of mine in the "Talk about" format:

"Talk about something you've learned from your relationships with other people."

"Talk about a life lesson you'll never forget, and what it has meant to you."

"Talk about homelessness, and how it has ever touched your life."

"Talk about who, and what, has made you the person you are today."

"Talk about your relationship to politics."

"Talk about war, and peace."

"Talk about your contribution to your world."

"Talk about how your cultural background has given you identity and strength."

"Talk about your most memorable spiritual experience."

"Talk about your life experiences with 'Awe.'"

"Talk about feeling like an object of prejudice, and what this was like for you."

"Talk about how your life in any way been a 'search,' and not."

"Talk about one dream that did not come true in your life, and another that did."

"Talk about what you still want in this lifetime that you don't already have."

"Talk about an experience that marked your transition into adulthood."

"Talk about two things you would change about our world."

Any of these self-disclosure items can lead into larger issues and topics for dialogue. They all place an emphasis on discovery and reflection, not on persuading others to agree. They're not stopping places, but leaping off places from which further *shared inquiry* can proceed, yet in a mood and tone of "to-me-ness" rather than as formal position statements to be argued. We're exploring each person's "personal reality" as they experience it, but not then attempting to have it foisted upon anyone else, understanding that there are as many "personal realities" as there are persons.[1]

Again, I don't go out of my way to invite my dialogue students to jump into "hot-button" topics like political differences, religious differences, racial issues, ethnic differences, gender issues, sexual orientation differences, different views on abortion, and so on. As soon as anyone sounds too dogmatic and absolutist on any one of these topic areas, persons who disagree will find it tempting to negatively disagree, dismiss, and diss. We've all of course been there, seen that, felt that.

So in learning dialogue, we don't go out of our way in early and middle stages to choose "hot-button" topics that are highly likely to trigger other peoples' defensiveness as soon as sites of disagreement are located.

---

1. See Rogers, *A Way of Being*, Ch. 5.

Especially not prior to first building a solid dialogue container across time, strong enough to safely contain and survive emotional and conversational intensities. Ultimately, dialogue can certainly include confronting differing beliefs and values and practices in an atmosphere of "loving struggle,"[2] but this is best saved for when all participants are fully prepared for it and up to it. Most of us are not yet there; that's down the way. At this stage of our development we're aiming to elevate above divisiveness.

We proceed more softly and indirectly for now, and this can be profound in and of it itself. It can take us further overall than heated discussion and debate, though there is a time and place for that as well. But not in the early phases of building our dialogue container with our **WEG-VIBES** practices. We need to first well-construct our containers, for everything will depend upon exactly this.

The "Talk About" items can be posed to individual partners within a pair format, or to a gathered dialogue group. In the group setting they could be addressed in either a circular one-at-a-time format, or to the group entire with individual volunteer respondents, depending upon group size, time constraints, and other factors.

In a larger dialogue group of twenty people or more I often use a "talking stick" (or other object), and each person responds to our inquiry when the "talking stick" reaches them. They are asked to be concise, taking a minute or two each (or longer in smaller groups). No one else is to interrupt the speaker, ask questions, or comment. We patiently hear from one participant at a time, each in turn, until we've passed our "talking stick" around our entire circle.[3] Then, if we choose to and there's time, we can process some of what we feel, have gained insight into, and wonder.

As an alternative to the above "Talk about" format, we can use verbal invitations that are slightly more developed, and that often end with a question mark:

"What's your continuing debate with today's world? How hard has it been for you to be involved in this debate?"

"Speak of the 'part' (the individual) and the 'whole' (the bigger than all the 'parts'): what has been the nature of the relationship between 'parts' and 'whole' in your life, and how has this changed across time?"

"To you, what is 'Holy' and 'Sacred'"?

2. Gordon, "Karl Jaspers, Dialogical Communication," 89–107.
3. Gordon, "Wisdom Circle Process."

"Recall a time when you wanted to share something with another person, but chose not to. How do you feel about this today, and what did you learn from that experience?"

"Think about saying 'Yes' to life versus saying 'No.' When was your hardest time saying 'Yes'? The easiest? What have you learned overall about saying 'Yes' and 'No' to life?"

"Remember a time in your life where you stifled your *Genuine Voicing*. What was this like, how did it feel, what did you learn? Then recall a time when you finally found and expressed your *Genuine Voice*. What happened? Any images / metaphors come to mind?"

"In what do you have 'faith'? Does your 'faith' vacillate, or remain fairly steady? When your 'faith' slips at times (if it does), how do you bring it back?"

"Speculate on your 'minimum daily requirement' of attention, and where this need gets met across a typical week in your current life. What do you see to be the role of giving and receiving attention in human life in general?"

"Let's dialogue about 'hope' and 'courage,' and the role they've played in our lives, and their place in life in general: where do you want to start?"

"When you come closer to seeing another person more as *Thou* and less as an *It*, how do you go about making this shift of perception? What can you tease-out as you reflect upon this?"

"For you, who or what is the ultimate 'Higher Power' or 'God'?"

Or, we can phrase our inquiry without a question mark:

"Let's reflect on the way 'suffering' has come to us in this life, how it has affected our life, and what we've gained from 'suffering.' And then let's dialogue on the meaning of 'suffering' across time in this world of ours, and maybe raise some related questions."

"It's been said and found that having a sense of humor is very important in life, that it's crucial to the art of living well. Let's dialogue about humor in our own lives, and humor in life writ large, and see what we can discover."

"Think of a time you had a conflict that ended up making you a better person, and exactly why and how that resulted, and share this story with us."

"Tell us a bit about 'interconnectedness,' and any thoughts or experiences you've ever had that suggest to you that things are more systemically interconnected than meets the eye."

Here's another workable format, the fill-in-the-blank template question:

"What can you say about the role of _____ in your life?"

"What can you say about the role of _____ in human life, as you see it?"

Possible topics are "love," "cooperation," "kindness," "courage," "sadness," "anger," "negativity," "positivity," "religion," "spirituality," "conflict," "peace," "justice," "self-control," "contentment," "happiness," and so on. When time is an issue, this format about *"the role of"* can help keep the length of responses within bounds.

Sometimes we can offer incomplete sentences that are about our **WEG-VIBES** dialogue practices themselves, and ask for completion. I usually have each person respond six times to the same single item, privately in writing, then in pairs have each person read their half-dozen responses to one or more partners, who then delve into whatever occurs to them. Then in a larger group setting we reflect upon some of what arose. Here are some incomplete sentences I've used:

"If I want to be seen as *Warm, Empathic, and Genuine,* then I . . ."

"When I am *Being Now and Here,* I . . ."

"The thing that most concerns me about making myself *Vulnerable* is that . . ."

"If I talked less and listened to others even more, then I believe . . ."

"When I'm blocked from finding and expressing *Genuine Voice* . . ."

"When I do find and express my *Genuine Voice* . . ."

"If I trusted the emptiness . . ."

"If I listened for the distant thunder . . ."

"If I saw *Empathic Listening* as a gateway, and listened more expansively . . ."

"If I were to listen more from the open spaces within my web of thoughts . . ."

The following percentage format can also be useful, asking first that a single incomplete sentence be privately responded to in writing a half-dozen times. Then, in pairs or small groups, each person's six written responses to that single item are shared, and explored:

"If I were to be 5-10 percent more self-aware each day . . ."

"If I were to give 10-15 percent more *Warmth, Empathy, and Genuineness* to myself, then . . ."

"If I were 5-10 percent more *Imaginative and Improvisational* in my life, then . . ."

"With 5-10 percent more *Suspending* skill, I could . . ."

"If I became 5-10 percent more aware of my breathing, then . . ."

"If I emptied 10 percent of my cup of tea . . ."

Another tremendous way to jumpstart a dialogue, one of my very favorites, is to have each person write a haiku poem about a common topic. So if the topic agreed upon is "*death*," or "*God*," or "*infinity*," or "*immortality*," or "*freedom*," or "*hate*," or "*greed*," or "*honesty*," or "*loneliness*," or "*success*," or whatever, then five minutes are given for each person to write a three-line poem consisting of five syllables on the first line, seven syllables on the second, and five syllables on the third line. The poem does not need to rhyme, but it could, up to the discretion of the poet.

So here is what I just now, in three minutes, came up with on "infinity": "More than I can think / More than I can ever know / True Grandness Supreme." After we've all finished writing, we have a "go-around," and each person reads their haiku aloud, one, two, three, sometimes four times, as we need. We spend time responding to each and every haiku, publicly sharing any images, associations, ideas, affirmations, and feelings that come into our minds as we hear these haikus. We *play* with, and off of, these responses, opening to our *stream of consciousness* and giving voice to what's passing through.

We dialogue playfully with each haiku. We're in no hurry here. We celebrate the inventiveness of each participant, finding material in their haiku to pay tribute to. There is more than initially meets the ear, so we slow down, we welcome silences, and allow heartfelt responses to gradually arise. We of course remember to quietly take four deep breaths, in and out, as we *Slow Down, Stand Back,* and *See More,* and as we then *Step Forth Wisely.*

When we're done with all of our haiku sharing, we might have an exploratory collaborative conversation about whatever came up overall, with no one taking any single stance too rigidly. Our words are shared lightly, tentatively, not in a tone of advocacy but in a spirit of appreciation, fondness, and fun. We allow our inquisitiveness to come to the fore, our wonder and delight.

This haiku poetry writing and sharing activity is a beautiful way to touch the heart as well as the mind, and I most highly recommend this approach. We don't have to be polished poets to write some pleasing haiku poems that can have us responding and reflecting together.

In sum, there's no shortage of ways to begin dialoguing. Dialogue can begin spontaneously from random comments and topics that get raised in everyday casual conversation, or we can use more structured methods in a group setting, or when otherwise appropriate. Responding to book materials, quotations, questions, using an incomplete-sentence format, writing and responding to haiku poems, all are great ways to go. They're workable means of inviting self-disclosure, *Vulnerability,* and reflection, and can be healthy dialogue starters, places from which we initiate our journey into *shared inquiry.*

And of course we lead, accompany, and follow with our **WEG-VIBES** practices all along the way. These are our guidelines, our compass, and they steer us rightly as we return to honoring them in action.

Taking Action

Be on the lookout for good sentence-completion possibilities all around you, good questions, quotes, and for "Talk About" topics. And don't short-change the charm of the haiku poem as a dialogue-starter, so simple in structure yet often packed with power of the best sort. These are ways to dialoguing.

Actively gather tools for getting dialoguing underway, not only because they can come in handy but because this collection process can become an exhilarating enterprise in and of itself. So snoop around, keeping your eyes and ears attuned to possible dialogue-starters for now or later. There's fun and meaning to be had in this endeavor.

Minimize looking for "hot-button" topics for now. Think about how you can more gently approach sensitive areas in a softer, less direct fashion, one more likely to elicit meaningful and healthy *personal* contributions rather than argumentative *position* statements. In the long run, more gets accomplished this way than with premature head-on confrontation. Our aim is to build a safe and strong dialogue container, to promote self-disclosure, to build trust, and engender intimate bonds of inter*personal* connection and community.

We have nobler ambitions than sponsoring a free-for-all fight club. The world needs fewer people fighting, and more people listening to their fellow human beings with human caring and understanding in their hearts. May we contribute to the cultivation of healing connective tissue among human beings, not to the further spreading of divisive slash and burn. Let us first connect and restore, and later we can pursue loving dialogical struggle as needed.

Human dialogue is our destination: the time for disclosing, connecting, bonding, and wondering is at hand.

Reflecting

My sense of curiosity is aroused, I'm wanting to find ways to stimulate sharing, inquiry, and discovery. Finding effective ways to welcome others into safe shared inquiry becomes my pleasure. I understand that inquiry for its own sake, and not only as a means to an immediately practical end, can itself bring satisfying contentment. We don't need finalized answers as much as significant questions worthy of calm contemplation, and I continue to further appreciate the wisdom of this realization.

17

Mental Warm-Ups

DIALOGUE INVOLVING TWO PEOPLE usually begins naturally and with no formal type of warm-up. But if we're initiating or facilitating a more structured dialogue group session, especially when highly creative thinking is our project, then group warm-ups can help us break the ice, establish preliminary bonding within our group, and get our brains and mouths moving. Warm-ups are optional, but in intentionally *generative* dialoguing where we're deliberately setting out to develop a range of images, free associations, and provocative possibilities, mental warm-ups can get our brains thinking divergently and provide a head start to the *generative* dialogue for which we're hoping.

When our target is to have highly inventive dialoguing with a lot of material generated, then we'll want to be specializing in what pioneering creativity expert Edward de Bono referred to as "Green Hat" thinking, symbolizing fertile growth, the outpouring of a full crop of fresh images, ideas, and possibilities.[1] We'll want a timeout on wearing other-colored hats that represent argumentativeness, criticality, skepticism, disapproval, domination, sarcasm, egotism, punishment, and so on. In daily life we get to see and hear from people invisibly wearing those other hats often enough, and for present purposes we're going to be wearing our invisible "Green Hats."

But research shows that between 60 percent to 80 percent of people are uncomfortable at first to put on "Green Hats" and go ahead and indulge in lateral *playful* thinking. Most people are used to thinking literally and somewhat straight ahead (or so they believe), "a-to-b-to-c," rather than divergently, meaning off-the-top and off-the-wall. So if we're hoping to be have a *generative* dialogue session where "Green Hat" divergent thinking and mental associating is our objective, then we might want to do some brief opening creativity exercises to prime the pump. Prominent leadership

1. De Bono, *Lateral Thinking*.

professor Warren Bennis once wrote that "Optimists have a sixth sense for possibilities that realists can't or won't see."[2] Sometimes for dialoguing we'll want to optimistically prime our sixth sense for possibilities.

Mental priming for *generative* dialoguing can include, in doses of a minute or two, a standard divergent thinking task of looking for three connections between any two things that at first seem unrelated, like *toothpaste* and *rap*; or *love* and *Swiss cheese*; or *work* and *sleep*; or *night* and *day*; *near* and *far*; *artificial intelligence* and *depression*; *dogs* and *spaceships*. Searching for such connections can be one way of beginning to put on our "Green Hat."

We might ask everyone to spontaneously give *Genuine Voice* to whatever they can come up with in a minute on each of the following: what are some of the ways a *tree* and a *flagpole* are alike? A *door* and a *tooth*? An *iguana* and a *pencil*? A *cat* and the *breeze*? Or, what are some of the other uses that *toothpaste* can be put to? A five-pound *dumbbell*? A *paper clip*? A used *milk carton*? What could be the advantages of having *three arms* instead of *two arms*? *Seven* toes instead of *five*? Life in a *parallel* (but different) *universe*? No wrong answers, and efforts rewarded with praise. "Green Hats" on yet?

And/or we can spend one minute visually looking around the room where we're meeting and notice any one of the following themes, before moving onto the next, for a total of three items in three minutes: *colors, angles, shapes, sizes, movements, variations, textures, points of contact*, and *mood tones*. After, we can talk about our experience of doing this (i.e., we *process* it), identifying how it was easy and difficult to do, and what recognitions it leads us to.

To tune-up the visual imagination we could ask our dialogue folks to close their eyes and mentally visualize a specific room in their house, to see the *floor*, the *ceiling*, the *walls*, the *windows, window coverings*, the *doors*, the *furniture*, the *personal artifacts*. In their mind's eye they're to run their imagination across these surfaces and objects. Then they're asked to take their mind into a different room, and proceed again. Ask them to look around in those rooms when they get home and see what they missed, added, changed. Ask them to repeat this activity three times this week on their own. What effects does this have on their visual memory? What benefits come from doing this? Does it help us to breathe and *Slow Down*, to breathe and *Stand Back*, to breathe and *See More*, to breathe and *Step Forth Wisely*?

2. Bennis and Townsend, *Reinventing Leadership*, Ch. 7.

Put Your Mother On the Ceiling is a delightful small book of children's imagination games written by psychologist Dr. Richard De Mille. One of his many games, "Being Things," involves pretending we're being different living and non-living things in our imaginations, and can be of some value as a dialogue warm-up even for adults.[3] As a short version, just to give you the flavor, let's start by having you be a *hummingbird* in your imagination for a few seconds. Now be a *pig*. Next be an *eagle*. Be a *duck*. Now a *tiger*. Now be a *giraffe*. Be something *swimming*. Be something *lying down*. *Standing* up. Be something *hot*. *Cold*. Be a *tree*. Be *yourself*. Be *someone else*. Now what do *you* want to be? Next be a *rock*. Be the *moon*. Be a *volcano*. Be *nothing*. Now what would you like to be? Even a couple of minutes of doing this game gets the "Green Hat" more comfortably situated on our head. This can be a fun game to do with a dialogue group.

Or, for a different kind of idea-starter exercise, we could give our group four letters (for example: g, t, b, w) and ask each person to write down and then orally share a sentence where each word begins with each of those letters in sequence (for example: g, t, b, w = "giant turtles break waves"). Let these shared sentences become a field of *play* for the group to romp in for two or three minutes together. We relax, we break the ice, we loosen, we *play*. I used this one last night, with success. It primed the pump, it got us to put on our "Green Hats."

Or, for three minutes we can have everyone write down all the words they can think of that start with the letter "d" (or any other letter). Then, for another three minutes we have the group sort the responses into two or three categories using some rationale or set of criteria. Then for a final three minutes we abandon those categories and come up with two or three different categories. Next, we talk about what the group experienced doing this.

Or, for one or two minutes let's identify all the "*round*" things in the world that we can. For another minute or two, how about "*square*" things? Now how about all the "*spiral*" things? After these few minutes, what does it do to our mind to use it like this? How does it feel *not* to have our mind doing this now? What *is* our mind doing now?

As we participate in our main dialogue we want to be totally receptive to mental images and associations and thinking that gets triggered within us, and also asking ourselves, "What other *images, ideas, metaphors, words, sounds*, could be brought in here? What existing elements could be replaced? Rearranged? Reversed? Combined? Tweaked and twisted?" Asking

3. De Mille, *Put Your Mother on the Ceiling*, 150–53.

warm-up questions can help set the tone so that we can then provocatively ask "What if . . . ?" rhetorical questions during our actual dialogue.

We could also ask each person in our dialogue group to be responsible for coming into a future session with a short creativity warm-up activity that they themselves have located or devised. This democratizes our warm-up, and further invites fun and unpredictability into our midst. I don't regularly use all of the above divergent thinking warm-up techniques in my own dialogue groups, though I have used each of them before, and do believe such devices can be of value.

As I've said earlier, my own favorite way to start a dialogue is simply with a brief "check-in" and "go-around." Other times I might have someone open a book I've written that contains over seven hundred brief entries and have them randomly turn to any page and read aloud any few sentences found there.[4] We then respond off the top, playing with what we hear. We riff, we jam, we spin our "Green Hats."

As we do so, it's always useful to breathe and *Slow Down,* to breathe and *Stand Back,* to breathe and *See More,* and to breathe and *Step Forth Wisely.* This helps ready us for our planned dialogue topic or assigned reading for the day.

Taking Action

If warming up yourself and/or others makes sense, try a few of the above. They can bring a mood of lightness to a group, they can get us laughing, and this broadens and builds our mental outlooks and resources. But if these tools sound too gimmicky, skip them. I do recommend periodic check-ins and go-arounds, however. These are dialogue mainstays and they yield info, provide release, promote caring, set people in motion, and can become a secure and comforting ritual.

Reflecting

Many of us have seen the bumper-sticker that says, "Minds are like parachutes, they only function when OPEN." When has my mind been most OPEN, and how has that been for me and others? How can I start to safely OPEN my mind during dialogue? Can doing mental warm-ups allow my creativity to

4. Gordon, *Actualizing.*

start to flow? What other creativity tools can I come up with and turn to, devices and methods that will prime my creative juices to flow? Am I willing to open my chute, and jump?

18

Returning to Awareness of Process

As you well know by now dialogue is not about advocacy, or competing sides locked in opposition, or battle and survival of the fittest. In dialogue we're not out to "attack" and "defend," and we're not speaking to, or in behalf of, any group of constituents.

Open-ended *person-centered* dialoguing is about embarking on a journey of *shared inquiry*, about disclosing and feeling and thinking and wondering together and experiencing and enjoying all this along the way, as well as where it takes us.

Later we can resort to *advocacy* of specific positions and proposals if that be appropriate, or pass along our ideas to those whose role it might be to discuss and debate these ideas more analytically and critically.

But we're dialoguing for now, we're persons on a scouting tour together, a wide-open hunt for seeds of potentiality. There are times when we need to set strategic persuasion efforts to the side and just plain meander, reflecting out loud more largely, originating new thinking together in an ambience of play and serendipitous potential. What eventuates for us will be more bountiful because of our time spent wandering and wondering this way, the way of dialogue.

We progress past the boundaries of what we think we know and peek at what else might also be. We courageously make more permeable our edges, and become eager explorers, declaring less and together digging for more. We become Indiana Joneses, probing for clues, inspirations, leads, the unknown. We know that enthusiastic excavations will occur as we delightedly dig together. Shoulder-to-shoulder we stand beside one another on a treasure hunt without a map, and no definite picture of precisely what our treasure will be.

This is the way of dialoguing: 1 + 1 = 3. You, me, and we, leading ourselves to the compounded benefits that accrue from our mixture of two, or ten, or twenty dialogue partners. Our **WEG-VIBES** model is our roadmap to dialogue, this is how we get there. Before our dialoguing even begins we would do well to explicitly remind all our dialogue partners of the **WEG-VIBES** practices that we're each striving to embody in our actions. We want to get our dialogue partners on the same page as to the importance of these core practices.

If each of our dialogue partners is committed to returning again and again to implementing the **WEG-VIBES** practices during our *shared inquiry*, then we're heading toward *person-centered* dialoguing. If one or more participants are not on board, our overall likelihood of success will take a hit, so it's time to again get everyone committed to working together. Dialoguing works best when all parts of the system are fully functioning, and intent upon collaboration.

To return to a recognition of our **WEG-VIBES** practices amid the twists and turns of our dialoguing takes mindful *self-awareness*. We will want to see what we're doing, and not doing, in these vital areas of dialogue practice. As Dr. R.D. Laing once put it: "The range of what we see and do is limited by what we fail to notice. And because we fail to notice that we fail to notice, there is little we can do to change until we notice how failing to notice shapes our thoughts and deeds."[1]

In each of our eight **WEG-VIBES** practice areas we can periodically lose vision. We can become blind to how much or how little we're talking and disclosing, whether we're overprotecting ourselves from risk, how present we are in the moment, to what extent we're emptying our cup, and all the rest. This is normal and to be expected, we can predict that this will happen. When it does, the challenge is to regain *self-awareness*, and then return to greater *self-management* within our **WEG-VIBES** areas of practice. We stray, and we come back. As Loch Kelly has put it: "We learn to return, and train to remain."[2]

This can be done. This is the work and way of dialogue.

Celebrated psychologist Dr. William James, one of the fathers of American psychology, wrote that "The faculty of voluntarily bringing back a wandering attention over and over again, is the very root of judgment, character, and will."[3] Sometimes we'll get so absorbed into the topic of our dialoguing that our awareness will stray from mindfully observing

1. Laing et al., *Interpersonal Perception*, Ch. 1.
2. Kelly, *Effortless Mindfulness*, 23.
3. James, *Essays and Lectures*, Ch. 4.

ourselves and our partners and how we're all doing in the **WEG-VIBES** practices. So close to the topic itself, the tree immediately in front of us, we lose sight of the surrounding patterns.

In addition to learning to repeatedly return to our own mindful *self-awareness*, directly communicating with our dialogue partners about how we've *all* been doing together in the **WEG-VIBES** areas makes good sense. So once our dialogue is over, we talk together about how skillfully we've all been in putting our **WEG-VIBES** practices into play. This is called *processing* our dialogue. We might want to do this at times during our dialogue too, but immediately following our dialoguing is a customary and opportune time for this. *Processing* our dialogue can take from five to fifteen minutes, depending on our group size.

We stand back from our dialogue topic itself, and we publicly reflect upon our practicing of **WEG-VIBES**. Did we each contribute to creating and maintaining an atmosphere of *Warmth* (i.e., *Caring, Accepting, Respecting,* and *Prizing)*? When did we show *Empathy*, and when did we not? How did everyone do with finding and speaking their *Genuine Voice*? To what extent did we each choose to make ourselves *Vulnerable*? Were we able to surrender sole allegiance to rational and logical thought and also open ourselves to *Imagination and Improvisation*? To what degree were we *Being Now* and *Here* in the present-centered moment? Did we earnestly strive for *Equality of Participation*, and reach it, and sustain it? How about our extent of *Suspending*, as compared with defending?

Talking about all of this and more, truthfully saying what we saw and experienced during our dialoguing, is how we further refine our **WEG-VIBES** practices. *Processing* is not always easy to manage, however, because we can accidentally slip back into talking about our dialogue topic itself. We'll need to remind one another that *processing* our **WEG-VIBES** practices is now our task at hand, our topic itself is for now behind us, so we let it go and leave it be.

This public *processing* of our dialogue is not always comfortable to do, but it can be done. *Meta-communicating* is a technical term that means "to be communicating about our own communication." As we pursue the way of dialogue we'll want to learn to *meta-communicate* with others, to be reflecting and communicating about our dialogue *process* itself, since this accelerates our development in the art of dialogue.

Dr. Carl Jung said this about our human capacity to "reflect" on something: "Reflection should be understood not just as an act of thought, but rather as an attitude. It is a privilege born of human freedom . . . It should, therefore, be understood as an act of *Becoming Conscious*."[4] As we publicly reflect about how we're each and all handling the elements of dialogue we foster everyone's growth toward becoming more fully *Conscious*. This can be daunting, of course, since it requires *Genuineness* and *Vulnerability*.

In this brief volume you've been invited to shine the light of your *awareness* upon our **WEG-VIBES** practices, to bring them out of the shadows and into the light of day. From hidden to found, from darkness to vision, to see with greater clarity what we and others are doing and not doing, and to openly communicate together about this. This is an ongoing task, never a totally done deal.

Self-awareness, self-management, and both using and publicly processing our use of **WEG-VIBES** and refining accordingly, this is what we do. This is our learning method and how we advance in an overall positive upward spiral.

But right now it's once again time to deeply breathe in, and out, and to *Slow Down*; and then to breathe in and out again, and *Stand Back*; and now to savor breathing in, and out, as we *See More*; and we celebrate our perseverance as we comfortably breathe ourselves into *Stepping Forth Wisely*. Good for us, good for others.

Joseph Campbell in speaking of the hero's journey observed that we're called to adventure and new horizons many times our lives, and that "Each time, there is the same problem: do I dare? And then if you do dare, the dangers are there, and the help also, and the fulfillment or the fiasco. There's always the possibility of a fiasco. But there's also the possibility of bliss."[5]

You are on yet another hero's journey. May blissful moments be yours in the weeks, months, and years to come as you accept this deeply profound call to adventure: pursuing the way of dialogue.

Taking Action

Stay conversant with our **WEG-VIBES** model as you continue ahead with your life. Allow it to flash into your mind at times and assist you in assessing your own and others' daily conversations. Use the *Dialogue Observation Guide* that follows to guide your self-observations of your own dialoguing, and your observations of others' attempts at dialoguing. Jot down key

4. Jung, *Memories, Dreams, Reflections*, Ch. 7.

5. Campbell, *Pathways to Bliss*, 133.

words to allow you to remember what you see. Then directly share and *process* these impressions with your dialogue partners, and ever strive to return to **WEG-VIBES**.

Being a student of human communication is a lifelong endeavor, so let this continue to be a high priority zone of learning going forward. Your personal and professional lives are at stake, and upgrades you make will definitely have payoffs. People will notice and be positively impacted by your heightened awareness and constructive communication choice-making. Of this, there is no question.

Thomas Merton once observed that "Life curves upward to a peak of intensity, a high point of value and meaning, at which all its latent creative possibilities go into action and the person transcends himself or herself in encounter, response, and communion with another." Merton goes on to note that it is for these that we have come into this world: communion, and self-transcendence.[6]

Dialogue serves both.

Usually when decrepit structures are chipping off and crumbling all around us, when they're downright hazardous structures in which to remain, we look for alternative structures that will be safer to inhabit. Therefore, again I say: welcome to the way of dialogue, and may it come to feel more and more like home, and where you're greeted by both communion and self-transcendence.

Reflecting

Now that I'm familiar with the core elements of dialogue, to what extent am I willing to commit myself to practicing WEG-VIBES in my shared inquiries with other people? On a good day, what level of overall commitment am I willing to make to the way of dialogue: 20 percent? 35 percent? 50 percent? 65 percent? 80 percent? 100 percent? On a not-so-good day? And on the not-so-good days, how I will I bring myself back yet again to the way of dialogue? One way always available to me is to breathe, Slow Down, Stand Back, See More, and Step Forth Wisely, for this way is always right under my nose.

6. Merton, *Love and Living*, 26-27.

Dialogue Observation Guide

WARMTH: *Unconditional Positive Regard, Caring, Accepting, Respecting, Prizing.*

How much Warmth is in the air, as opposed to Coldness? Are Warm words exchanged, and Warm nonverbal behaviors shown? Is this Warmth sustained, or intermittent? How is Caring evident, how is Respect apparent? Is there a tone of Acceptance in the room, rather than rejection? In what ways is Prizing manifested and felt? Does everyone get to benefit?

EMPATHY: *Deeply Understanding One Another's Frame of Reference, from Heart and Head.*

To what extent are people "getting" one another? Do they seem to be on the same "wavelength"? Are they moving into the heart of mutual under-standing together? Can people see and feel what others are trying to get at? Is this understanding made apparent, and experienced by all? Are paraphrasing and questions of clarification actively present?

GENUINENESS: *Authentic Voice, Honesty, Sincerity, Congruence with Self and Others.*

Are people being honest and real with one another, and in a caring man-ner? Is there withholding that obstructs forward progress, or are people step-ping up and saying what they actually think and feel? Is this honest voicing being sustained throughout the inquiry, or does it come and go? Do any truly courageous exemplars emerge as truth-telling heroes, as way-showers? On a scale of 1 – 100, how would this dialogue be rated on Genuineness?

VULNERABILITY: *Willingness to Emotionally Risk, Courage in the Pres-ence of Fear.*

Are the dialogue participants playing it too safe, or are they taking risks and making themselves Vulnerable? Is it one step forward and two steps back, or is there continuing momentum? How widespread is this risk-taking? Where else does it need to occur? Does the risk-taking productively serve the Whole? Is an atmosphere of overall safety and security present as well?

IMAGINATION AND IMPROVISATION: *Creativity, Playfulness, Mental Spontaneity.*

How creative are people being? Are they reaching for newness? Who is actively and consistently drawing upon their Imagination? Are people having fun being Improvisational, are they taking themselves and one another by surprise? Does the group get stuck in this area, and if so, what can they do about it? Describe this group in terms of its overall "playfulness." Are any fresh terms or images or ideas getting created, is there an upward spiral of creation?

BEING NOW AND HERE: *Present-Centeredness, Engaged Embodiment, Mindfulness.*

Do people seem to be daydreaming, or talking too much about the past or future? Do they appear deeply engaged in this alive present moment? Is there an air of vitality, is there "electricity" in the room? At what moments does the group feel most present-centered? Do you believe that centered breath awareness and mindfulness are being practiced? Are silences bringing people more fully into Now and Here?

EQUALITY OF PARTICIPATION: *Inviting Equal Talk-Time, Support-Responding.*

Is there Equality of Participation in this interaction? Who is perhaps taking too much talk-time, and who too little? How is this affecting the balance and flow, and the overall dynamics? Is shift-responding being used rather than support-responding? Are nonverbal attention-giving behaviors strongly present? What further refinements of participation frequency are needed? Are we verbally inviting others to enter into the dialogue, and sincerely making space for them to do so? Are silences broken prematurely, and by the same persons each time?

SUSPENDING: *Lightly Holding Opinions and Positions and Judgments and Reactions.*

Are people more lightly holding their beliefs, opinions, judgments, positions? Are they softening their grip? Are they willing to put some space around their own thoughts and positions, making more room for fresh additional thinking to also enter in? Do they work at repairing lapses in Suspension, opening themselves to greater internal spaciousness so that thinking can move more freely? Are they welcoming wise and healthy "don't know" mind by emptying their cups?

Synthesis

What are the participants in this attempt at dialogue doing especially well: what are their top one or two or three WEG-VIBES practices right now?

Where could they do better: are they stuck or limited anywhere? On what one or two or three WEG-VIBES practices do they most need to up-level their choices and refine their actions?

How would this dialogue effort be informally "graded" or rated in each of the WEG-VIBES practices, or overall?

What three words first come to mind to describe this particular journey toward shared inquiry?

Putting the pieces together, and being honest, what can we learn for the future from this specific excursion?

Acknowledgments

I FIRST OF ALL want to thank my many University of Hawai'i—Hilo students, past and present, for giving me so much of yourselves across the decades. I've known faculty who've counted the years and days until retirement yet this has never been my own personal experience because, my dear students, being with you gives core meaning to my existence. I continue to enjoy and celebrate you each and every session, and semester, and decade. You've been unpretentious, utterly genuine, and deeply human. The most diverse student body in America (it's a fact), you've been willing to share your stories in our classes to let us know what you've been through, what your confusions and fears are, what your personal victories have been, what makes you different, and what we all share in common. You've clearly shown that *person-centered* dialoguing works, and reaffirms our humanity. And I look forward to my future students who have yet to arrive: let's make something good happen.

Aloha extends from my heart to all of you dear former students as well from the University of Hawaii at Manoa, Texas A&M University, the University of Nebraska at Omaha, Iowa Western, Metro Tech, West Valley College, Cal State Humboldt, the University of Kansas, and San Jose State. You too have added greatly to my life, and I thank you.

My sons Deva and Drew, you are among my very closest confidants and buddies in this world, and I greatly value our relationships and our communication. I have always been totally glad to be your dad, and this will never change. And my daughter Liahna, you're my longest-term friend on the planet, and I continue to treasure our deep and abiding connection. With all three of you wonderful beings, Deva, Drew, and Liahna, our lively and mutually respectful dialoguing streams onward, and I'm extremely grateful for our free and open communication. I love each of you tremendously, always know this.

My precious wife Laylai, you are my sweetheart and daily companion in life, and you bring much joy and love and firm ongoing foundation. My stepson Ranu, I'm delighted to see our communication beginning to take flight. You and your mom both make "home sweet home" feel especially comfortable, warm, and cozy.

Friends and professional colleagues Gay and Noelie, you are my closest working allies, and each of you strengthens, counsels, and shows me how to Be. You are extraordinary women, professionals, and persons. I thank you Gay for being an exemplar in illustrating how to consistently treat others with *Warmth, Empathy,* and *Genuineness.* I am deeply honored to be your friend. And I respect you Noelie for, among other things, unrelentingly doing all you can to save the world; you are among the most dedicated on the planet, and humble us all. You are a gem of a human being.

My UH-Hilo Department of Communication colleagues Iva, Yoshi, Jing, Rayna, Kalama, Randy, Steve, and Colby, we comprise a harmonious and persevering departmental team, and I'm glad to be a member of our well-rounded and competent faculty line-up.

To my dear Division of Humanities colleagues, you are a wonderful group of talented and good human beings to be among, and you enable a fun and delightful workplace.

Carl Rogers, you've been a steadfast beacon for me, as has your powerful *person-centered* approach that is so central to interpersonal communication and dialogue. Martin Buber and Karl Jaspers, you are among my other main dialogue heroes, and you've touched my mind and life. I've never met Bill Isaacs but I've used his dialogue book for fifteen years in my dialogue course. To you Bill I owe much, and to your own mentor, David Bohm, whose influence amply permeates these pages. And within my own national academic discipline of Communication I recognize Richard Johannesen, Ken Cissna, Rob Anderson, Ronald Arnett, Bud Goodall, John Stewart, and Leslie Baxter, for each of you has played a role in attempting to take dialogue out of our discipline's shadows and bring to dialoguing its due attention. Kudos for your important pioneering work and voices.

Others with whom I've personally enjoyed communication and dialoguing across time include Steve, Glen, Phil, Karman, and Jiajia. I consider each of you a trusted and valued friend, and our communication has been a highlight through the years.

I'm thankful to Wipf and Stock for accepting the initial proposal for this work, and that it has now emerged as a WS Resource Publication. The world definitely needs an increase in healthy dialoguing, and you dear publisher know this and care enough to support the present effort. I much appreciate you bringing this work to a public readership.

To the readers of this book, from the Big Island of Hawai'i please let me extend a warm Mahalo to you for being responsive to some of what's in this volume and making your world more satisfying for you and others to inhabit.

Aloha to All as we move into the third decade of the twentieth century, striving for ongoing high-quality communication that elevates and unites human beings on this Earth.

Bibliography

Abram, David. *Becoming Animal: An Earthly Cosmology*. New York, NY: Vintage, 2010.
———. *Spell of the Sensuous*. New York, NY: Vintage, 2017.
Achenbach, Joel. "Growing on You." *National Geographic* (November 2005) 19.
American College Health Association. *National College Health Assessment 2017*. https://www.acha.org./NCHA.
Anderson, Rob, et al., eds. *Dialogue*. Thousand Oaks, CA: Sage, 2004.
——— et al., eds. *The Reach of Dialogue*. Cresskill, NJ: Hampton, 1994.
Auden, W.H. AZQuotes.com. https://www.azquotes.com/quote/352152.
Baas, M., et al. "A Meta-Analysis of 25 years of Mood–Creativity Research." *Psychological Bulletin* 134 (2008) 779–806.
Barfield, Gay Leah. "Evolution of Person-Centered Encounter: Creating Egalitarian Environments for Mattering, Meaning and Healing." *Person-Centered & Experiential Psychotherapies* (2019). http://doi.org/10.1080/14779757.2019.1650809.
Baxter, Leslie. "Communication as Dialogue." In *Communication: Perspectives on Theory*, edited by Gregory Shepherd et al., 101–09. Thousand Oaks, CA: Sage, 2006.
Baxter, Leslie, and Barbara Montgomery. *Relating*. New York, NY: Guilford, 1996.
Baxter, Leslie, and Dawn Braithwaite, eds. *Engaging Theories in Interpersonal Communication*. Thousand Oaks, CA: Sage, 2008.
Bennis, Warren, and Robert Townsend. *Reinventing Leadership*. New York, NY: Morrow, 1995.
Berger, Peter, and Thomas Luckmann. *The Social Construction of Reality*. New York, NY: Vintage, 1966.
Bohm, David. *On Dialogue*. London: Routledge, 1997.
———. *On Creativity*, edited by Lee Nichol. New York: Oxford University, 1996.
Bowlby, John. *A Secure Base*. Boston, MA: Basic Books, 1988.
Brach, Tara. *True Refuge*. New York, NY: Bantam, 2016.
Bradley, Omar. AZQuotes.com. https://www.azquotes.com/quote/1101143.
Brady, Mark. *The Wisdom of Listening*. Boston, MA: Wisdom, 2003.
Brown, Brene. *Dare to Lead*. New York, NY: Random House. 2018.
———. *Daring Greatly*. New York: Gotham, 2012.
Brown, Stuart. *Play*. New York, NY: Penguin, 2009.
Brown, Kirk, et al. *Handbook of Mindfulness: Theory, Research, and Practice*. New York, NY: Guilford, 2015.
Buber, Martin. *Way of Man*. New York, NY: Citadel, 1995.
———. *I and Thou*. Translated by William Kaufmann. New York, NY: Charles Scribner, 1970.

———. "Elements of the Inter-Human." In *Bridges Not Walls*, 5th edition, edited by John Stewart, 450–60. McGraw-Hill, NY: 1990.

Campbell, Joseph. *Hero with a Thousand Faces*. New York, NY: Pantheon, 1949.

———. *Pathways to Bliss*. Novato, CA: New World, 2004.

Campbell, Joseph, and Bill Moyers. *The Power of Myth*. New York, NY: Doubleday, 1988.

Carson, Shelley. *Your Creative Brain*. San Francisco, CA: Wiley, 2010.

Chan, Wing-Tsit. *Way of Lao Tzu*. New York, NY: Macmillan, 1963.

Cissna, Kenneth, and Rob Anderson. "Communication and the Ground of Dialogue." In *The Reach of Dialogue*, edited by Rob Anderson et al., 9–33. Cresskill, NJ: Hampton, 1994.

——— and Rob Anderson. "Contributions to Carl Rogers to a Philosophical Praxis of Dialogue." *Western Journal of Speech Communication* 54 (1990) 125–47.

——— and Rob Anderson. "Theorizing About Dialogic Moments." *Communication Theory* 8 (1998) 63–104.

Cuddy, Amy. *Presence*. New York, NY: Little, Brown, and Co., 2015.

De Mille, Richard. *Put Your Mother on the Ceiling*. New York, NY: Viking, 1973.

Derber, Charles. *Pursuit of Attention*. New York, NY: Oxford University, 2000.

De Waal. *Age of Empathy*. New York, NY: Harmony, 2009.

Einstein, Albert. *Living Philosophies*. Simon & Schuster, 1931.

Epstein, Mark. *Thoughts Without a Thinker*. New York, NY: Basic Books, 1995.

Ferguson, Gaylon. *Natural Wakefulness*. Boston, MA: Shambhala, 2009.

Feynman, Richard. AZQuotes.com. https://www.azquotes.com/quote/824334.

Friedman, Maurice. *Martin Buber: The Life of Dialogue*. New York, NY: Harper and Row, 1955.

Garner, Alan. *Conversationally Speaking*. Boston, MA: Lowell House, 1997.

Gazziniga, Michael. *Human*. New York, NY: Harper Collins, 2008.

Gelb, Michael, and Sarah Caldicott. *Innovate Like Edison*. New York, NY: Penguin, 2007.

Gergen, Kenneth. *Relational Being*. New York, NY: Oxford University, 2009.

Gilbert, Elizabeth. *Big Magic*. New York, NY: Penguin, 2015.

Goleman, Daniel. *Focus*. New York, NY: Harper Collins, 2013.

Goleman, Daniel, and Richard Davidson. *Altered Traits*. New York, NY: Penguin, 2017.

Goodall, Jr., H. Lloyd, and Peter M. Kellett. "Dialectical Tensions and Dialogic Moments as Pathways to Peak Experiences." In *Dialogue: Theorizing Difference in Communication Studies*, edited by Rob Anderson et al., 159–74. Thousand Oaks, CA: Sage, 2004.

Gordon, Ronald. *Actualizing*. Bloomington, IN: iUniverse, 2011.

———. "America: Amused to Death." https://www.baltimoresun.com/opinion/op-ed/bs-ed-op-0831-amused-death-20180830-story.html.

———. "Beyond the Failures of Western Communication Theory." *Journal of Multicultural Discourses* 2 (2007) 89–107.

———. "Communication, Dialogue, and Transformation." *Human Communication* 9 (2006) 17–30.

———. "Global Empathic Consciousness Development." *International Journal of Journalism and Mass Communication* 3 (2016) 116–25.

———. "Karl Jaspers: Existential Philosopher of Dialogical Communication." *Southern Communication Journal* 65 (2000) 105–18.

———. *Tuning-In: The Art of Mindful Communicating*. Bloomington, IN: iUniverse, 2019.

———. "The Twenty-First Century Call of the Humanities in Asia and the Pacific: Educating the Human Heart." *Hawai'i Journal of Humanities* 1 (2019) 3-16.

———. "Water Metaphors in Traditional Chinese and American Thought." Paper presented at the Joint International Conference on Chinese Communication Studies, Xiamen University, Fujian Province, Peoples' Republic of China, 2005.

———. "The Wisdom Circle Process: Community, Story, and Spirit." In *Dialogue Among Diversities,* edited by Guo Ming Chen and William Starosta, 43–61. Washington, D.C.: National Communication Association, 2004.

Grant, Adam. *Give and Take.* New York, NY: Penguin, 2013.

Griffin, Em. *A First Look at Communication Theory.* 7th ed. New York, NY: McGraw-Hill, 2014.

Grigg. Ray. *The Tao of Zen.* Edison, NJ: Alva, 1999.

Haggbloom, S.J., et al. "The 100 Most Eminent Psychologists of the Twentieth Century." *Review of General Psychology* 6 (2002) 139–52.

Hahn, Thich Nhat. *The Art of Communicating.* New York, NY: Harper Collins, 2013.

———. *Breathe, You Are Alive.* Berkeley, CA: Parallax, 1999.

———. *Peace is Every Step.* New York, NY: Bantam, 1992.

Hasson, Uri. "Your Brain on Communication." https://www.tedtalks.com.

Hayes, Stephen, et al. *Acceptance and Commitment Therapy.* New York, NY: Guilford, 2012.

Herrigel, Eugen. *Zen in the Art of Archery.* Translated by R.F.C. Hull. New York: Vintage, 1999.

Hodes, Aubrey. *Encounter with Martin Buber.* New York, NY: Penguin, 1975.

Isaacs, William. *Dialogue and the Art of Thinking Together.* New York, NY: Doubleday, 1999.

Jackson, Phil, and Hugh Delehanty. *Sacred Hoops.* New York, NY: Hyperion, 1995,

James, William. *Essays and Lectures,* edited by Richard Kamber. New York, NY: Pearson, 2007.

Jaspers, Karl. *The Way to Wisdom.* New Haven, CN: Yale University Press, 1973.

Johannesen, Richard. "The Emerging Concept of Communication as Dialogue." *Quarterly Journal of Speech* 57 (1971) 373–82.

Jung, Carl. *Memories, Dreams, Reflections.* New York, NY: Vintage, 1965.

Kelley, Harold. "The Warm-Cold Variable in First Impressions of Persons." *Journal of Personality* 18 (1950) 431–39.

Kelly, Loch. *Shift into Freedom.* Boulder, CO: Sounds True, 2015.

———. *The Way of Effortless Mindfulness.* Boulder, CO: Sounds True, 2019.

Kirby, Gary, and Jeffery Goodpaster. *Thinking.* Englewood Cliffs, NJ: Prentice Hall, 1995.

Kouzes, James, and Barry Posner. *The Leadership Challenge.* 6th ed. San Francisco, CA: Jossey Bass, 2017.

Kornfield, Jack. *The Wise Heart.* New York, NY: Bantam Books, 2008.

Krishnamurti, J., and David Bohm. *The Ending of Time.* New York, NY: Harper, 1985.

Laing, R.D., et al. *Interpersonal Perception.* New York, NY: Harper & Row, 1966.

Luft, Joseph. *Of Human Interaction.* Houston, TX: Mayfield, 1969.

Matson, Floyd, and Ashley Montagu, eds. *The Human Dialogue.* New York, NY: Free Press, 1967.

Mayeroff, Milton. *On Caring.* New York, NY: Harper & Row, 1990.

Merton, Thomas. *Love and Living.* New York, NY: Farrar, Straus, and Giroux, 1979.

Moore, Thomas. *Education of the Heart.* New York, NY: Harper Collins, 1996.

Nepo, Mark. *The Book of Awakening.* San Francisco, CA: Conari, 2011.

———. *Seven Thousand Ways to Listen.* New York, NY: Free Press, 2012.

Nichols, Michael. *The Lost Art of Listening*. New York, NY: Guilford, 2009.

Niebauer, Chris. *No Self, No Problem*. San Antonio, TX: Hierophant, 2019.

Osborn, Alex. *Applied Imagination*. New York, NY: Charles Scribner Sons, 1963.

Palmer, Parker. *A Hidden Wholeness*. San Francisco, CA: John Wiley, 2006.

Paul, Richard, and Linda Elder. *Critical Thinking*. New York, NY: Pearson, 2019.

Porges, Stephen. *The Pocket Guide to Polyvagal Theory*. New York, NY: W.W. Norton, 2017.

Poulakos, John. "The Components of Dialogue." *Western Speech* 38 (1974) 199–212.

Prather, Hugh. *Notes to Myself*. Moab, UT: Real People Press, 1970.

Rifkin, Jeremy. *The Empathic Civilization*. New York, NY: J.P. Tarcher, 2009.

Rodriguez, Noelie, and Alan Ryave. *Systematic Self-Observation*. Thousand Oaks, CA: Sage, 2002.

Rogers, Carl. "Basic Conditions of the Facilitative Therapeutic Relationship." In *The Handbook of Person-Centered Counseling and Therapy*, edited by M. Cooper, et al., 1–5. New York, NY: Palgrave Macmillan, 2007.

———. *On Becoming a Person*. Boston, MA: Houghton Mifflin, 1961.

———. *The Carl Rogers Reader*. Howard Kirschenbaum and Valerie Henderson, eds. Boston, MA: Houghton Mifflin, 1989.

———. "Tentative Formulation of a General Law of Interpersonal Relationships." In Rogers, *On Becoming a Person*, 338–46.

———. *A Way of Being*. Boston, MA: Houghton Mifflin, 1980.

Rogers, Carl, and David Russell. *Carl Rogers: The Quiet Revolutionary*. Roseville, CA: Penmarin, 2002.

Sagan, Carl. *Cosmos*. New York, NY: Ballantine, 2013.

Salzberg, Sharon. *Lovingkindness*. Boston, MA: Shambhala, 1997.

Sardello, Robert. *Silence: The Mystery of Wholeness*. Berkeley, CA: North Atlantic, 2008.

Schumacher, E.F. AZQuotes.com. https://www.azquotes.com/quote/1198097.

Senge, Peter, C., et. al. *Presence*. New York, NY: Doubleday, 2004.

Shenk, Joshua Wolf. *Powers of Two*. Boston, MA: Houghton Mifflin, 2014.

Smalley, Susan, and Diana Winston. *Fully Present: The Science, Art, and Practice of Mindfulness*. Philadelphia, PA: De Capo, 2010.

Sorokin, Pitirim. *The Ways and Power of Love*. Boston, MA: Beacon, 1954.

Stephens, Greg, et al. "Speaker-Listener Neural Coupling Underlies Successful Communication." *Proceedings of the National Academy of Sciences* 107 (2010) 11425–4430.

Stewart, John, "Foundations of Dialogic Communication." *Quarterly Journal of Speech* 64 (1978) 183–201.

Stone, Douglas, et. al. *Difficult Conversations*. New York, NY: Viking, 1999.

Suzuki, D.T. *An Introduction to Zen Buddhism*. New York, NY: Grove Press, 1964.

Tart, Charles. *Living the Mindful Life*. Boston, MA: Shambhala, 1994.

———. *Waking Up*. Lincoln, NE: iUniverse, 2001.

Tepper, D., and R. Haase. "Effects of Nonverbal Communication of Facilitative Conditions." *Journal of Counseling Psychology* 25 (1978) 200–04.

Thunberg, Greta. *No One is Too Small to Make a Difference*. New York: NY: Penguin, 2019.

Turkle, Sherry. *Reclaiming Conversation*. New York, NY: Penguin, 2015.

Tolle, Eckhart. *A New Earth*. New York, NY: Penguin, 2006.

———. *The Power of Now*. Novato, CA: New World, 2004.

Van Der Kolk, Bessel. *The Body Keeps the Score*. New York, NY: Penguin, 2014.

Wagner, Jane. AZQuotes.com. https://www.azquotes.com/quote/611220.

Wald, George. "Life and Mind in the Universe." In *Essays on Science and Creativity*, edited by Diana DeLuca, 1–14. Honolulu, HI: HCTE, 1985.

Watson, Burton. *Chuang Tzu: Basic Writings*. New York, NY: Columbia University Press, 1964.

Wilhelm, Richard, and C. G. Jung. *The Secret of the Golden Flower*. New York, NY: Harcourt, Brace, 1932.

Williams, Paul. *Das Energi*. New York, NY: Electra, 1973.

Williams, Paul, and Tracey Jackson. *Gratitude and Trust*. New York, NY: Penguin, 2014.

Zimmer, Carl. "Genes are Us, and Them." *National Geographic* (July 2013) 102–03.

Zinn, Jon-Kabat. *Coming to Our Senses*. New York, NY: Hyperion, 2005.

About the Author

RONALD D. GORDON (PH.D., University of Kansas) is Professor of Communication on the Hilo campus of The University of Hawai'i. He teaches interpersonal communication, seminar in human dialogue, seminar in listening, and senior-level courses in communication and love, and leadership and communication.

Ron Gordon has been twice-nominated for the University of Hawai'i Board of Regents Excellence in Teaching Award, served for eight years as chair of his department, and for three years as President of the Pacific and Asian Communication Association. His scholarship has appeared in more than twenty different academic venues, including the *Journal of Multicultural Discourses, Journal of Business Communication, Communication Quarterly, Psychological Reports, China Media Research, Human Communication, Perceptual and Motor Skills, International and Intercultural Communication Annual*, and *Small Group Behavior*. His previous books are *Tuning-In: The Art of Mindful Communicating, Actualizing*, and *Communicating with the West* (published in Japan).

www.ingramcontent.com/pod-product-compliance
Lightning Source LLC
Chambersburg PA
CBHW070922270326
41927CB00011B/2688